CHINA

FOCUS ON FORTY YEARS OF REFORM AND OPENING-UP

百名摄影师聚焦中国改革开放四十年

CHINA DAILY
中国日报

中国文联出版社

在举国共庆改革开放四十周年之际，中国日报社策划推出这本《百名摄影师聚焦中国改革开放四十年》画册。从肩扛手搬、人工犁地播种到机械化作业、多样化经营，从向土地求生存到向海洋要资源，从物资短缺、市场抢购到物产富足、供销两旺，从城乡二元、“农民工潮”到城乡融合、乡村振兴，从民以食为天到文化生活丰富多彩、各民族传统文化大放光彩，从自行车王国到汽车大国，从绿皮蒸汽火车到拥有完全自主知识产权的“复兴号”中国高铁，从围观不同肤色的面孔到“中外一家亲”……这本画册通过精心筛选的300多幅摄影佳作，真实、生动、立体地展现我国改革开放四十年的伟大历程和辉煌成就，以强烈视觉张力的黑白光影来讲述中国故事，不仅记录了伟大时代的飞跃、社会发展的亮点，也折射出百姓生活的变迁。

以1978年十一届三中全会召开为标志，在中国共产党的坚强领导下，中国人民四十年改革开放，四十年众志成城，四十年春风化雨，四十年砥砺奋进，用双手书写了国家和民族发展的壮丽史诗。改革开放这场中国的第二次革命，不仅深刻改变了中国，也深刻影响了世界。

雄关漫道真如铁，而今迈步从头越。习近平主席在2018年新年贺词中指出，我们要以庆祝改革开放四十周年为契机，逢山开路，遇水架桥，将改革进行到底。站在新的历史起点上，让我们以新气象、新作为，勇担新时代“改革开放再出发”的历史使命，共同奏响新时代奋进最强音。

在此，感谢各位摄影家、各协办单位和各界人士对画册以及中国日报社的支持。中国日报社将与各界共同当好新时代改革开放事业的推动者、贡献者，做好新时代改革开放故事的记录者、传播者。

周树春
全国政协常委
中国日报社总编辑

周树春

This album celebrates the 40th anniversary of economic reform and opening-up, and is China Daily's salute to the ordinary Chinese people without whose painstaking efforts China would not be the country that it is today.

It is the contract responsibility system that was first tried out in a village in East China's Anhui province that blazed the trail of reform in rural China. The rural reform not only helped China produce more food for but also triggered the overall reform in Chinese society.

Skimming through this album, one can travel through the panorama of China's past four decades, witness how the country transformed from a land of bicycles into a nation of cars, how the gap between rural and urban areas has gradually narrowed, how the development of expressways and high-speed trains has boosted economic and social development, and how an underdeveloped country has become the world's second-largest economy.

These more than 300 photographs unfold, in different angles and dimensions, what the country has experienced and achieved in 40 years. Many black and white photos tell the story of a China that has seen the lives of ordinary Chinese undergo fundamental changes.

The Third Plenary Session of the 11th National Congress of the Communist Party of China in 1978 was a milestone. Since then the Chinese people, under the leadership of the CPC, have marched triumphantly ahead, overcoming even the most severe difficulties and sparing no efforts in writing a new chapter in the history of China.

Indeed, reform and opening-up have changed China; they have also changed the world.

In his 2018 New Year address, President Xi Jinping said: We should take the 40th anniversary of reform and opening-up as an opportunity to continue the social transformation, overcoming all stumbling blocks on the way. At the new starting point of history, we should shoulder the new mission of launching another round of reform and opening-up.

This album is a testament to the resolve of the Chinese people to chart a brighter future for the country. So no matter how difficult it is to cross the new pass — of a new round of reform and opening-up — they will press ahead on their journey till they achieve success.

The journey of this album would be incomplete without the efforts of the photographers. We applaud their devotion to their art and dedication to the cause of the people. And we appreciate the efforts of our partner units and the celebrities who have contributed to the publication of this album.

China Daily will continue to contribute its share to reform and opening-up, and record the events and achievements of the people on this journey toward a better future.

Zhou Shuchun

Zhou Shuchun

Editor-in-Chief of China Daily
Member of the Standing Committee of
the 13th National Committee of the
Chinese People's Political Consultative Conference

I

1979年，安徽省凤阳县，小岗村民严俊昌、严立学、严立坤站在自己承包的土地上。1978年11月24日，小岗生产队18户农民自发搞起了农业"大包干"，"交足国家的，留足集体的，剩下都是自己的"。沿着这个起点，整个中国的命运发生了历史性转折。

Villagers on their own contracted land in Xiaogang village, Fengyang county in East China's Anhui province, in 1979. It was the first village where arable land was contracted to villagers in late 1970s.

汪　强 / Wang Qiang

1979年初，山东省青岛市，兰山路礼堂里正在召开传达学习十一届三中全会精神的大会。

At a meeting where the decisions of the Third Plenary Session of the 11th National Congress of the Communist Party of China are being announced in Qingdao city, East China's Shandong province in early 1979.

任锡海 / Ren Xihai

1983年春，山东省青岛市崂山区雕龙嘴村，村民正在村干部的带领下丈量土地，实行土地承包。

Arable land is measured for villagers to contract their plots of land in Diaolongzui village, Laoshan district, Qingdao city of East China's Shandong province, in the spring of 1983.

任锡海 / Ren Xihai

1984年10月1日，北京，参加庆祝中华人民共和国成立35周年群众游行的北京大学学生，突然举出“小平您好”的横幅，兴高采烈地通过天安门广场。

Students with a banner bearing the words "Hello, Xiaoping" during the National Day parade in Beijing's Tian'anmen Square on October 1, 1984.

贺延光 / He Yanguang

1979年，河北省易县，农村的骡马大集，老乡们在等待着交易。

At a horse and mule fair in Yixian county, North China's Hebei province, in 1979.

王文澜 / Wang Wenlan

1984年7月2日，山西省朔县利民乡，当地传统庙会上，牲口交易人畜两旺。

贺延光 / He Yanguang

A cattle fair in Limin town, Shuoxian county, North China's Shanxi province, on July 2, 1984. The fair had just been restored after being suspended for many years.

1983年，云南省楚雄市，农村打谷场上劳作丰收的场景。

Villagers engage in collective production in west Yunnan province in 1983.

徐晋燕 / Xu Jinyan

2006年5月16日，山西省偏关县寺沟村，一户人家正在夯土建造的长城墩台下犁地、撒种，这里的多数年轻人都外出打工，妇女和年长的男人成了主要劳力。

赵　青 / Zhao Qing

A family working on its fields by the Great Wall at Sigou village, Pianguan county of North China's Shanxi province on May 16, 2006.

1979年秋，安徽省凤阳县小岗村，农民严宏昌用借来的拖拉机收获自家丰收的粮食。

汪　强 / Wang Qiang

In the autumn of 1979, a villager borrows a tractor to store the crop of his own rather than for the People's Commune as in the past .

1987年12月，四川省成都市，青城山附近的农田里，母亲带着年幼的孩子在地里劳作。

A youngster in fields in Qingcheng Mountain, Chengdu, capital of Southwest China's Sichuan province, in December, 1987.

王文泉 / Wang Wenquan

1982年，陕西省宝鸡市阳平镇，家庭联产承包责任制在农村实施后，往日打麦场上繁忙喧闹的集体劳动景象逐渐消失了，生产队用于扬场的大型风扇，如今在弃用时成为孩子们嬉戏的游乐器械。

Children having fun climbing up a deserted big farming tool at Yangping town, Baoji city of Northwest China's Shaanxi province, in 1982.

白　涛 / Bai Tao

1997年5月26日，河南省信阳市明港镇，农忙时节农民们在金色的田野里耕作。

高健生 / Gao Jiansheng

Villagers harvest wheat in Minggang town, Central China's Henan province, on May 26, 1997.

2016年10月18日，内蒙古自治区赤峰市克什克腾旗乌兰布统乡，一对夫妇正在自家承包的牧场上装运冬储饲料。

薛　为 / Xue Wei

A couple in Hexigten banner, the Inner Mongolia autonomous region, is reaping the grass in their own contracted grassland as fodder for cattle on October 18, 2016.

1992年，山西省平遥县，古城墙下农民赶集交易的市场繁忙有序。

At a rural commodity fair outside the city wall of Pingyao county, North China's Shanxi province, in 1992. Pingyao is well known for its old city wall.

刘　阳 / Liu Yang

2018年4月2日，四川省雅安市天全县思经乡，当地发展冷水鱼养殖。

刘祯祥 / Liu Zhenxiang

A good catch at a fish pond in Sijing town, Tianquan county of Ya'an city in Southwest China's Sichuan province, on April 2, 2018.

2018年6月18日，山东省荣成市，海带捕捞作业现场。荣成海带养殖面积、产量均居全国县级市第一位。

安菲菲 / An Feifei

A harvest of kelp in Rongcheng city, East China's Shandong province, on June 18, 2018. The county is known as the country's hometown of kelp.

1994年10月，西藏自治区曲水县拉萨河，一些乡镇的孩子们上学还用最原始的交通工具牛皮筏子渡河。

杨秉政 / Yang Bingzheng

Boarding a cowhide raft on the Lhasa River in Qushui county in the Tibet autonomous region in October, 1994. Such rafts were the main means of crossing the river then.

1996年，宁夏回族自治区，黄河岸边的大水车与渡河人们背着的羊皮筏子。 刘 雷 / Liu Lei

Men carrying sheepskin rafts below the waterwheel by the Yellow River in Ningxia Hui autonomous region in 1996.

1999年7月10日，海南省三亚市，经历短暂的休渔期后，三亚的大小渔船开足马力，一场捕鱼狂潮正在形成。

A fishing boat heads to Sanya city, South China's Hainan province, with its catch on July 10, 1999.

王景春 / Wang Jingchun

1983年，云南省德宏傣族景颇族自治州，在中缅边境瑞丽江上来往做生意的边民。

徐晋燕 / Xu Jinyan

Passengers use a ferry to cross the Ruili River, Southwest China's Yunnan province, in 1983. Residents started to do business across the border between China and Myanmar.

2018年2月12日，河北省保定市安新县圈头村，农户在结冰的荷塘里收获莲藕。

金　洁 / Jin Jie

A farmer harvests lotus roots in Quantou village, Anxin county, North China's Hebei province, on February 12, 2018.

2017年8月，广西壮族自治区北海市，这里的海滩保留了一种传统的采盐工艺，工人们每收完一次盐后要把残余晶体刮均匀，便于下一次结晶分布平衡，这是海盐的制作工艺流程之一。

Salt making on a section of beach in Beihai city, Guangxi Zhuang autonomous region, in August, 2017.

王辑东 / Wang Jidong

1986年4月，上海市，参加宝钢热轧厂施工立功受奖的青年突击队员们，当记者采访时，他们你推我让不肯拍照。

于文国 / Yu Wenguo

Outstanding workers pose for a photo, one of them with a little encouragement, for an interview in Shanghai Bao Steel in April 1986.

1981年8月21日，陕西省西安市，宝成铁路发生毁灭性的水害，西安铁路局职工徒步向完全瘫痪的宝成铁路线输送救援物质。

李少童 / Li Shaotong

Railway workers sending relief material by foot in suburban Xi'an, Shaanxi province, on August 21, 1981, after the railway was destroyed by floods.

1994年，陕西省西安市，西安铁路局凤州工务段白水江区段换枕木，闲歇空余中的工人群体。

白　涛 / Bai Tao

Railway maintenance workers have a break from their work changing the sleepers under the rail tracks in Fengzhou, Xi'an city, Northwest China's Shaanxi province, in 1994.

1995年，辽宁省阜新市，新邱露天矿矸子山上的捡煤女工们。

王玉文 / Wang Yuwen

Women workers at work at an open coal mine in Fuxin, Northeast China's Liaoning province, in 1995.

2010年6月6日，北京市房山区，鑫华双安煤矿的工人们在进行最后的作业。在这之后，北京全面关停煤矿，修复周边环境。

饶　强 / Rao Qiang

Miners at a coal mine in Fangshan district, Beijing, on June 6, 2010. Beijing planned to close all its coal mines then.

2013年3月28日，北京市房山区长阳镇，深夜，护路工人卖力地抢修水毁道路。

池　淳 / Chi Chun

Maintenance workers repair a road that was damaged by flooding in Changyang town, Fangshan district, Beijing, on March 28,2013.

2006年，北京市朝阳区，奥运场馆工地，建设国家体育场馆“鸟巢”的工人们在酣睡午休。

李英杰 / Li Yingjie

Migrant workers sound asleep after hard work at a construction site for Beijing Olympic Games in Beijing in 2006.

2018年4月20日，四川省成都市彭镇，几位正准备施工的电力工程人员。

钟永和 / Zhong Yonghe

Electric engineers chatting at Pengzhen town, Chengdu, capital of Southwest China's Sichuan province, on April 20, 2018.

2016年，吉林省长春市，中外合资企业一汽大众的装配车间生产线。

王玉文 / Wang Yuwen

A glimpse of an auto assembly line at First Automobile Works in Changchun city, Northeast China's Jilin province, in 2016.

2017年5月18日，四川省绵阳市，野马汽车制造厂里沸腾的车间。 郑玉德 / Zheng Yude

A glimpse of an auto works in Mianyang city, Southwest China's Sichuan province, on May 18, 2017.

2017年12月21日，吉林省长春市，吉林中车长春轨道客车生产线，技术人员做好全面质量把关工作。

Technicians are inspecting a high-speed train on the assembly line in Changchun, Northeast China's Jilin province, on December 21, 2017.

姜　建 / Jiang Jian

CRH380BL-5501

2014年8月3日，上海市浦东新区，陆家嘴金融贸易区高楼林立，工人们在为中国第一高楼——上海中心大厦，吊装最后一根钢梁。

黄伟国 / Huang Weiguo

The construction of Shanghai Tower is underway on August 3, 2014.

2018年6月27日，北京市昌平区，冬奥会举办地途经的兴延高速公路上，平阳坊镇史家桥段中跨施工现场。

王冀昌 / Wang Jichang

Expressway under construction for the Beijing Olympic Winter Games 2022 in Changping district, Beijing, on June 27, 2018.

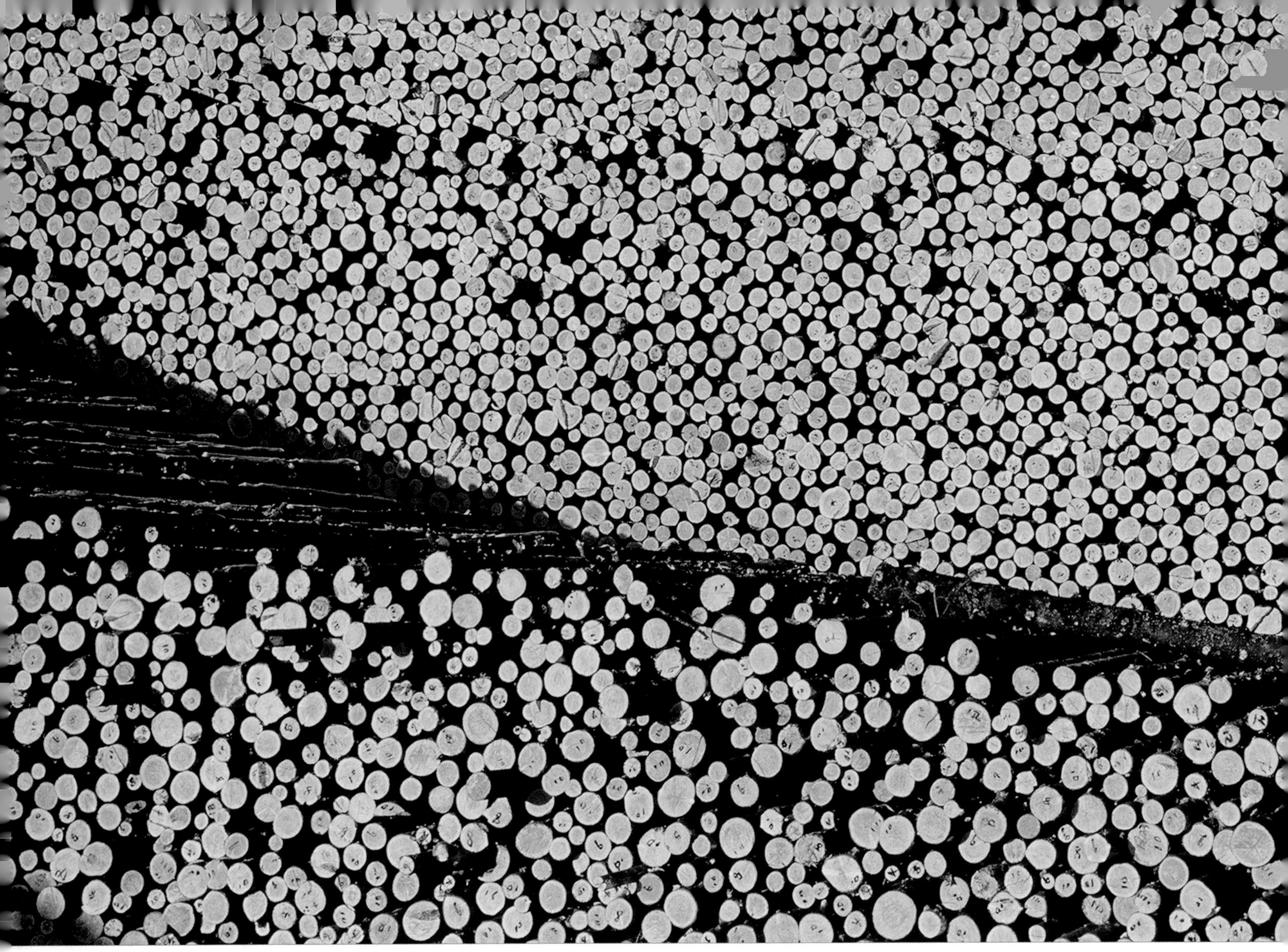

1986年12月，黑龙江省伊春市，朗乡林业局贮木场，林场工人在堆积如山的木材中工作。

Inspecting logs at a timber mill in Langxiang town, Yichun city, Northeast China's Heilongjiang province, in December, 1986.

谭景涛 / Tan Jingtao

2009年3月，新疆维吾尔自治区塔里木盆地，中国石油勘探队的队员们在进行油气勘探作业，这里无水、无电、无通讯信号，工作条件艰苦。

An oil exploration crew work at Tarim in the Xinjiang Uygur autonomous region in March, 2009. The working conditions there are harsh.

于文国 / Yu Wenguo

2016年5月19日，山东省济南市济阳县，电力工人高空作业。内蒙至山东1000千伏特高压输变电工程建成投产，电力由昔日的紧缺状态发展至今天能够满足国民经济需求。

Workers working high above the ground in Jiyang county, Ji'nan city, capital of East China's Shandong province, on May 19, 2016.

王　剑 / Wang Jian

投票箱

1997年，山东省青岛市，冠县路街道办事处举行换届选举大会。

An election is held for a new subdistrict office head at Guanxianlu subdistrict, Qingdao city, East China's Shandong province, in 1997.

任锡海 / Ren Xihai

1988年9月15日，武汉市青山区红钢城十一街，税务专管员吴彧年例行检查时，发现个体商贩漏税现象，令其补交。

许　林 / Xu Lin

A tax collector collects tax from a peddler selling beancurd in Qingshan district, Wuhan city of Central China's Hubei province, on September 15, 1988.

1988年9月10日，湖北省武汉市，市场出现抢购金首饰风潮，一位市民递进来一捆人民币，全部用于购买金项链。

许　林 / Xu Lin

To fight against inflation, people buy gold ornaments in Wuhan city, Central China's Hubei province, on September 10, 1988.

1981年，海南省陵水县，防疫人员在向黎族青年进行防御疟疾宣传，教她们用显微镜观察疟原虫。

黄一鸣 / Huang Yiming

Disease prevention workers let people see malarial parasites through a microscope at Lingshui county, South China's Hainan province, in 1981.

2017年3月31日，江苏省连云港市东海县石湖乡大娄村，村医王芳与乡防保所的医生和志愿者到村民家中，为村民提供健康服务。

蔡晓雨 / Cai Xiaoyu

A visiting doctor provides healthcare services for villagers on March 31, 2017.

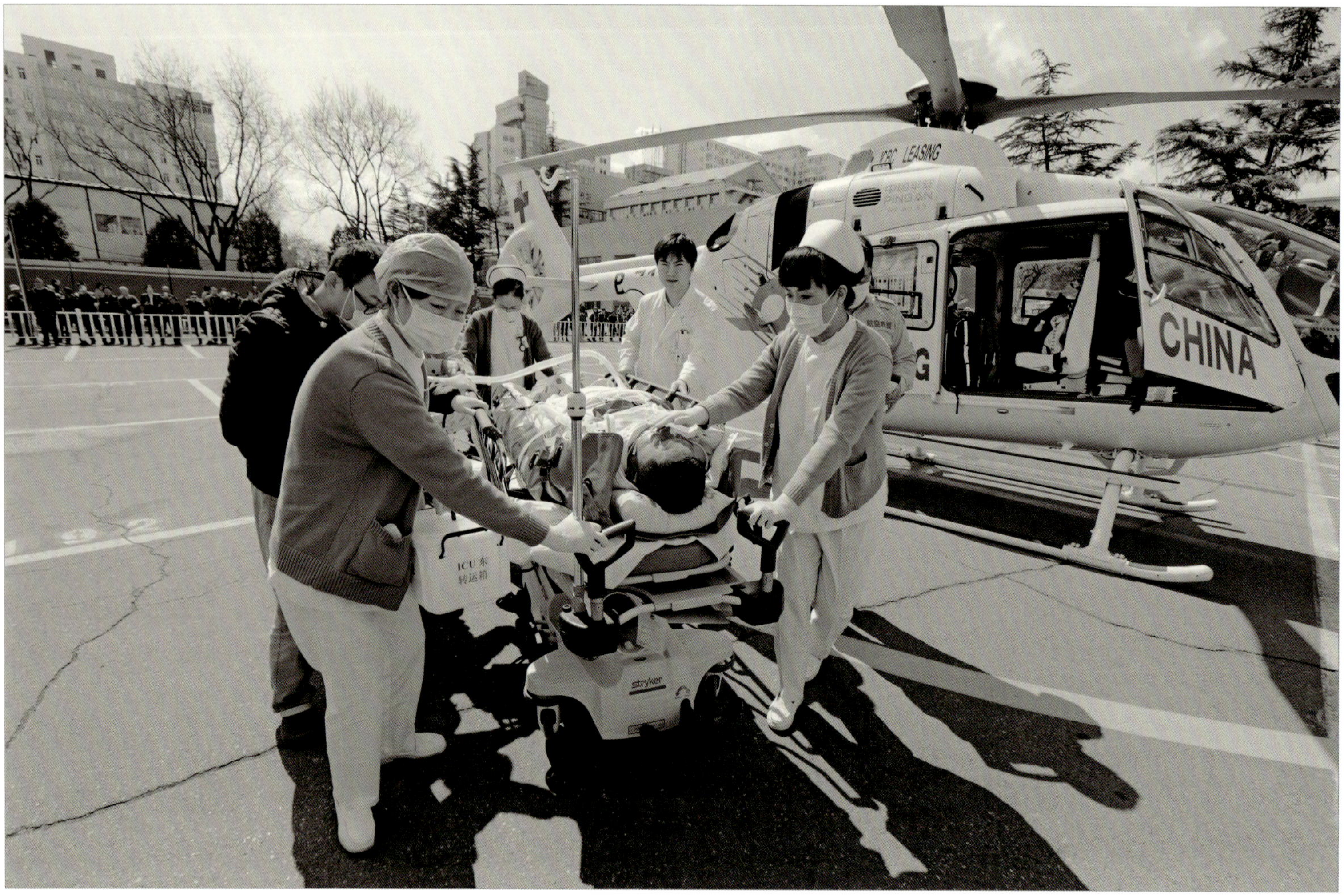

2017年3月26日，北京市朝阳区，一名呼吸危重症患者通过直升机转运至中日友好医院进行紧急抢救治疗。

朱兴鑫 / Zhu Xingxin

A helicopter sends a patient in serious condition to the China-Japan Friendship Hospital in Chaoyang district, Beijing, on March 26, 2017.

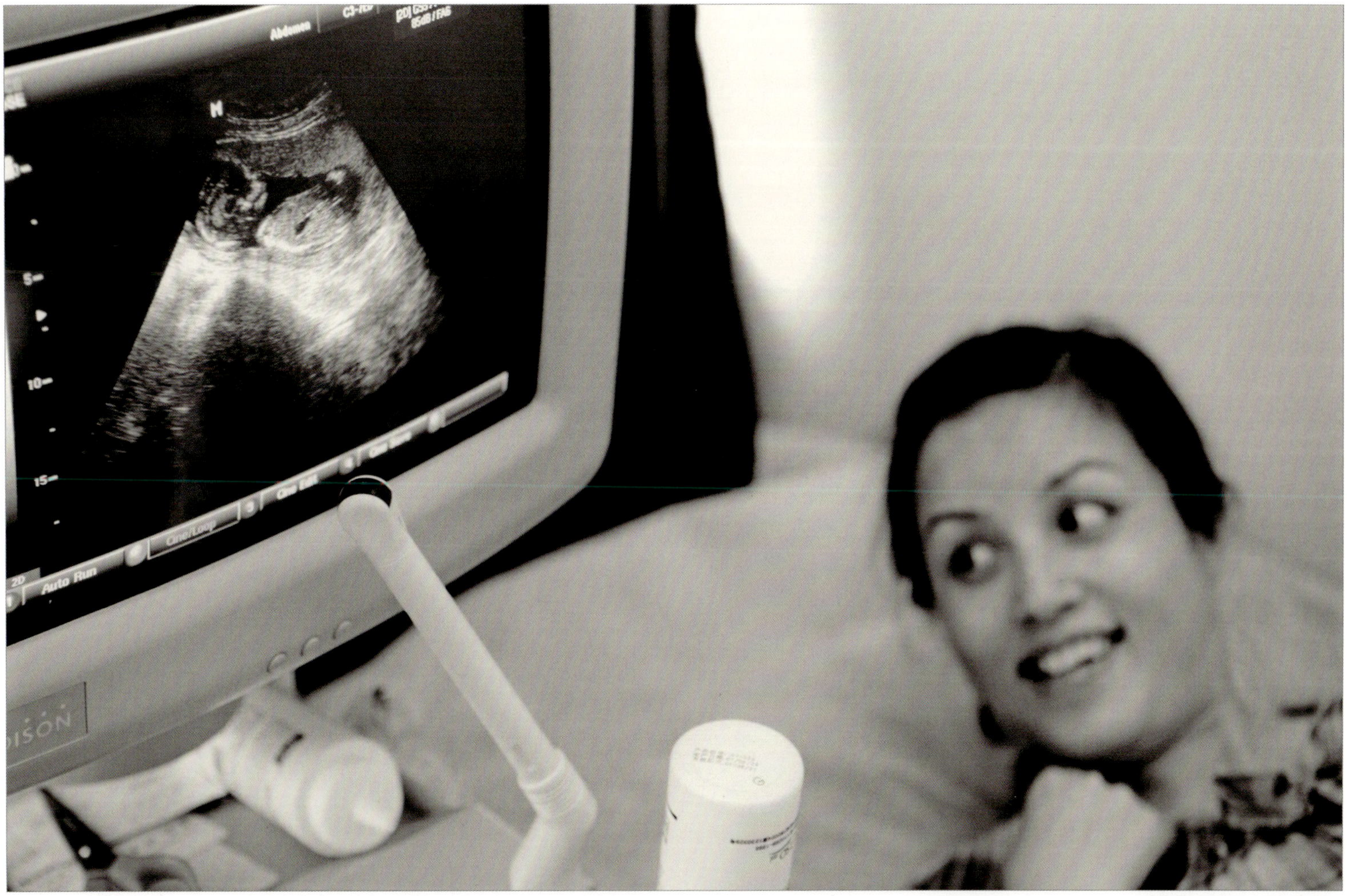

2009年6月14日，上海市，一位患有子宫肌瘤的准妈妈，经过中医药调理成功怀孕，孕检时她在B超室迫不及待地起身观看四个月大的胚胎宝宝。

张　明 / Zhang Ming

A pregnant woman tries to look at her four-month-old fetus on B-ultrasonic screen on June 14, 2009. It is a traditional Chinese medicine therapy that has made it possible for this woman who has hysteromyoma to conceive a baby.

2008年6月25日，四川省汶川县索桥村，老汉王云金抚摸着自家门牌述说地震灾难。

李振盛 / Li Zhensheng

Villager Wang Yunjin from Suoqiao village, Wenchuan county of Sichuan province, talks about how devastating the earthquake was on June 25, 2008. His village was destroyed in the quake.

2008年5月21日，四川省绵竹市广济镇新和村，大地震后，村民吴金莉在自家废墟上梳妆打扮。

Villager Wu Jinli making up in the ruin of her home after an earthquake in Xinhe village, Guangji town of Mianzhu city in Southwest China's Sichuan province, on May 21, 2008.

张　风 / Zhang Feng

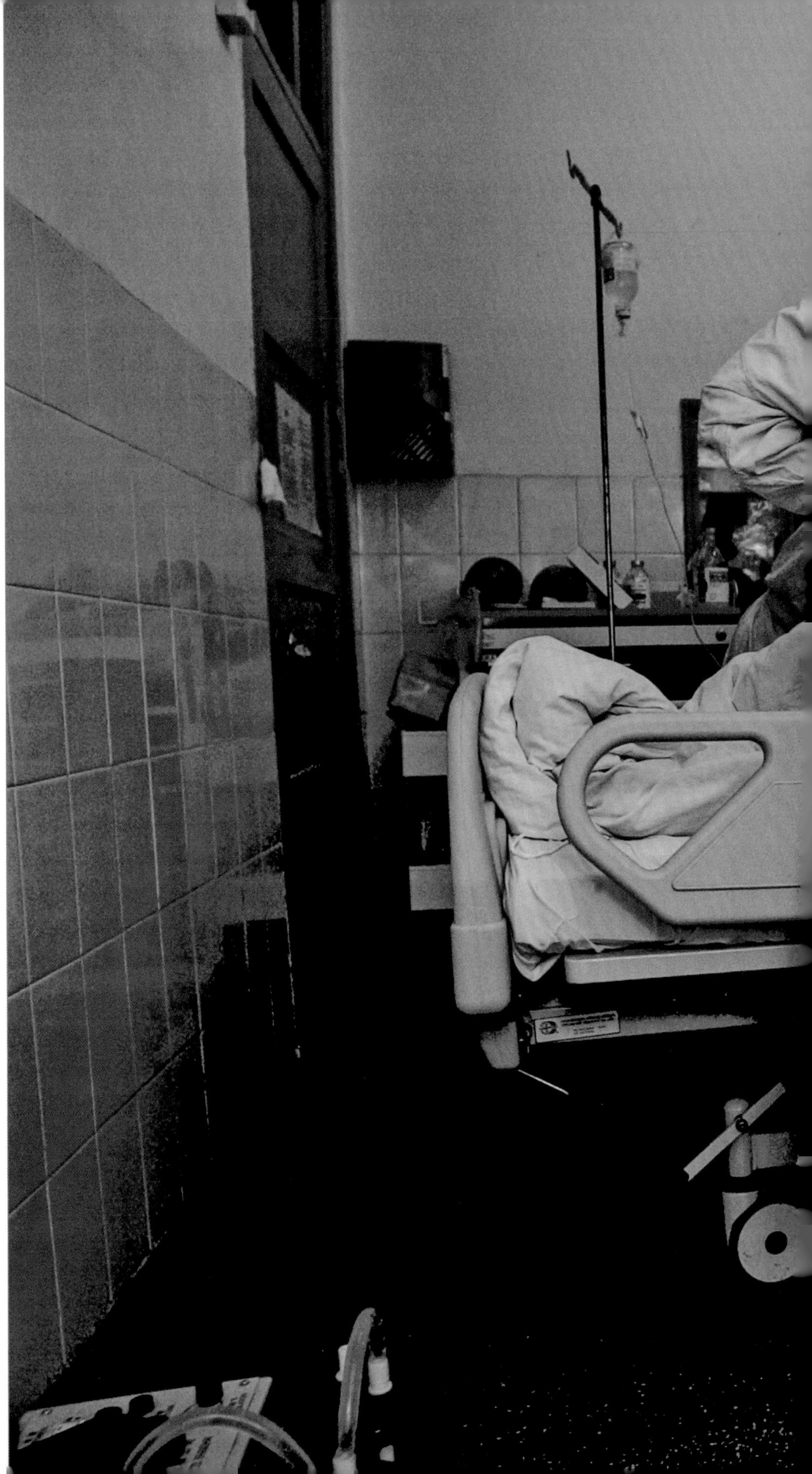

2003年4月30日，北京地坛医院，一位SARS患者经抢救无效不幸死亡，一位医生久久地站在他的遗体旁。

A doctor stands before a SARS victim at Beijing Ditan Hospital on April 30, 2003.

贺延光 / He Yanguang

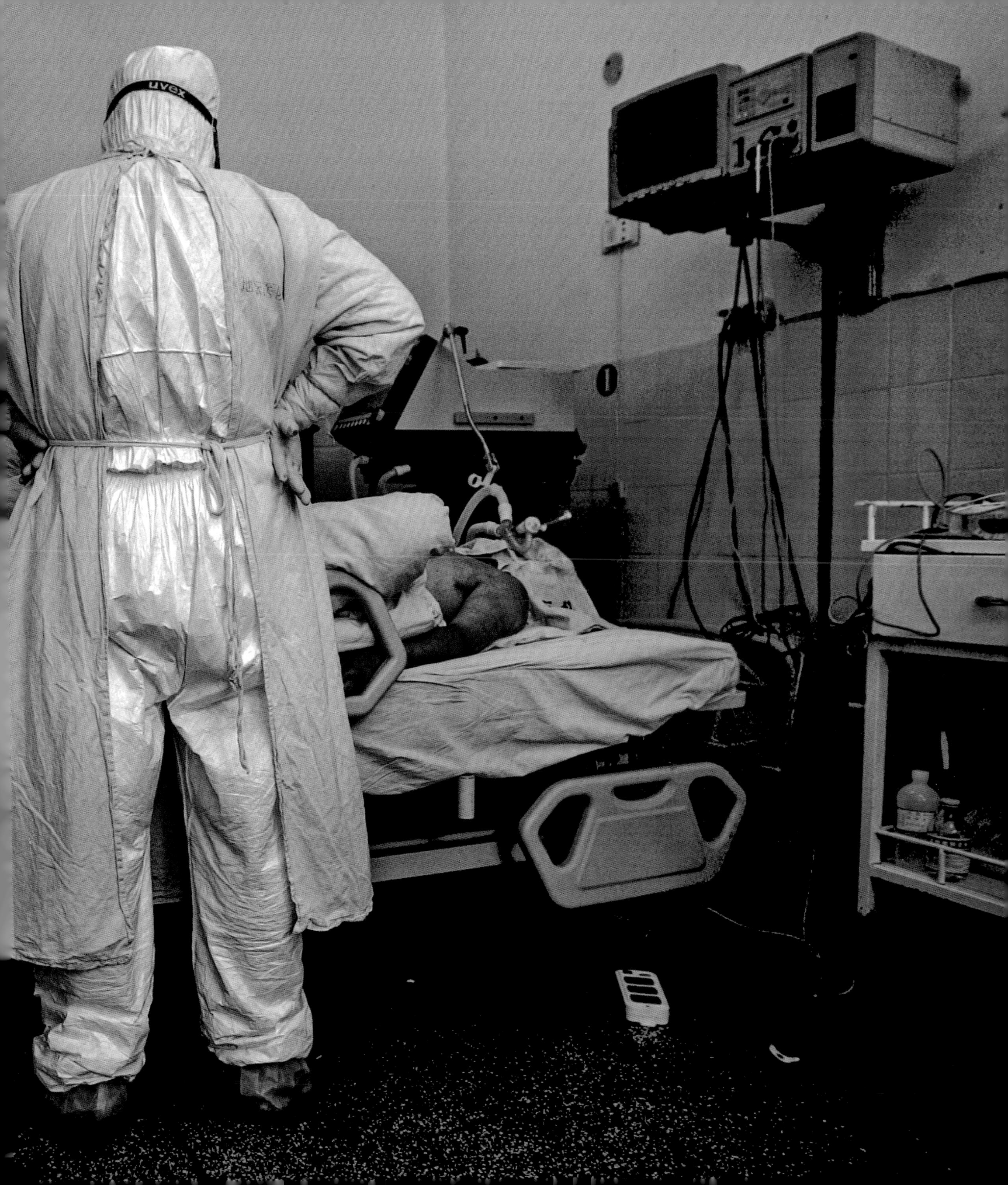
uvex

2018年7月2日，内蒙古自治区阿拉善地区，75岁的王天昌是甘肃省武威市凉州区长城乡红水村村民，他带领老伴及家人在腾格里沙漠治沙种树8000亩，历时长达19年。

任世琛 / Ren Shichen

Seventy-five-year-old Wang Tianchang watering a plant in a desert in Alax League on July 2, 2018. He and his family have planted trees and grass in desert for 19 years and turned about 530 hectare of desert into oasis.

2016年8月8日，青海省可可西里国家级自然保护区，保护区的工作人员拦截住过往车辆，保护迁徙期间的藏羚羊过青藏公路。

顾　莹 / Gu Ying

Trucks and travellers are stopped for Tibetan antelopes to cross the road in Hoh Xil, West China's Qinghai province, on August 8, 2016.

2001年4月14日，河北省丰宁满族自治县，1000多位来自北京的市民在植树固沙时突遇七级大风。

张 风 / Zhang Feng

Beijing residents planting trees at Fengning Manchu autonomous county, North China's Hebei province, on April 14, 2001. The county about 100 kilometers north of Beijing is one of the major sources of sandstorms.

2007年5月17日，北京市密云区，工人们铲收草坪后工间休息，忽然一阵风吹过，扬起满天黄沙。

黄冠海 / Huang Guanhai

Workers take a break after digging up turf in Miyun county, Beijing, on May 17, 2007.

2007年9月18日，内蒙古呼伦贝尔市，满洲里边防西乌珠尔站，护线守边的一家人在落日余晖里归来。

A soldier with his family at a border station in Manzhouli city of North China's Inner Mongolia autonomous reigon on September 18, 2007.

骆　飞 / Luo Fei

2017年4月，江苏省连云港市，消防支队的战士们在进行爬楼训练。

Fire fighters training in Lianyungang city, East China's Jiangsu province, in April, 2017.

黄志琴 / Huang Zhiqin

2016年8月22日，北京市怀柔区，装备学院的教官在给参加军训的中学生们示范标准的俯卧撑动作。

A drillmaster showing students how to do push-ups at Huairou district, Beijing, on August 22, 2016. The middle school students were doing military training.

王宇澄 / Wang Yucheng

2015年3月，上海市，龙华烈士陵园，清明节前，复员退伍军人祭扫牺牲的战友。

鲍国良 / Bao Guoliang

Veterans meet at Longhua Cemetary for Revolutionary Martyrs in Shanghai after paying tribute to the tombs of their commrade-in-arms in March, 2015.

2015年9月3日，北京天安门广场，纪念中国人民抗日战争暨世界反法西斯战争胜利70周年大会在北京隆重举行，受阅部队威武雄壮。

Military troops in formation for a parade on the 70th anniversary of the victory of the Chinese People's War of Resistance against Japanese Aggression (1931-45) and the Anti-Fascist War in Beijing on September 3, 2015.

李　舸 / Li Ge

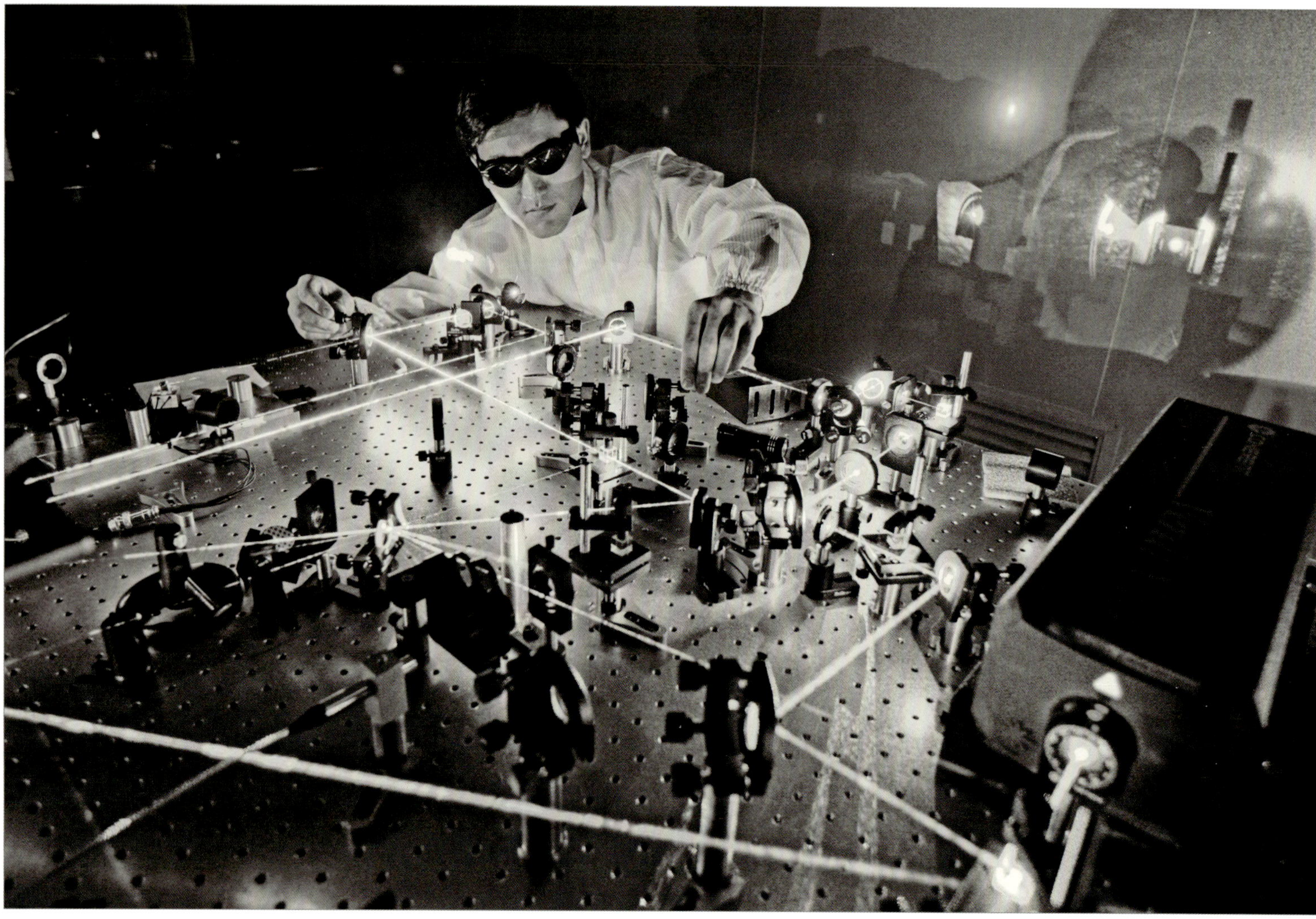

2011年，湖南省长沙市，国防科技大学量子计算实验室科研人员进行激光稳频试验。

乔天富 / Qiao Tianfu

An experiment underway at a quantum lab in National University of Defence Technology in Changsha city of Central China Hunan province, in 2011.

2007年5月19日，山东省淄博市，医生用世界尖端的质子技术为患者治疗肿瘤。 钱 捍 / Qian Han

A cancer patient receives treatment in Zibo city, East China's Shandong province, on May 19, 2007.

2009年6月13日，陕西省西安市，暂停24年后重启的临潼兵马俑1号坑第3次发掘再次震动世界。

An archaeologist at an excavation site of terra cotta warriors in Xi'an, Northwest China's Shaanxi province on June 13, 2009 when the No 1 pit of terra cotta warriors was dug for the third time.

黑　克 / Hei Ke

2015年9月23日，江西省南昌市，考古人员在现场清理汉代海昏侯墓车马坑。

郭　晶 / Guo Jing

An archaeologist at an excavation site at Nanchang city of East China's Jiangxi province on September 23, 2015. It is the tomb of a prince of the Han Dynasty (206 BC-220 AD).

2010年3月15日，福建省福州市，长乐国际机场首次开通福州至台北桃园机场的空中直航航班。

祝敏松 / Zhu Minsong

The first flight from Taoyuan Airport in Taiwan lands at Fuzhou Changle International Airport in Changle district, Fuzhou city, East China's Fujian province, on March 15, 2010.

1984年10月1日，北京天安门广场，建国35周年国庆观礼的一位港澳代表，手捧鲜花国旗，爱国之情溢于言表。

A compatriot from Hong Kong and Macao delegation at the Great Hall of the People in Bejing on October 1, 1984.

王文泉 / Wang Wenquan

2011年10月16日，广东省广州市海珠区，中国进出口商品交易会吸引成千上万来自世界各地的采购商汇聚于此，选购中国制造的各种产品。

A glimpse of the Import and Export Commodities Fair in Guangzhou, capital of South China's Guangdong province, on October 16, 2011.

刘冬平 / Liu Dongping

出口 Exit
出口 Exit
Westin Pazhou
Area C, Hall 16.2

2001年7月13日，北京市，国际奥委会主席萨马兰奇宣布北京获得2008年奥运会主办权之后，市民们走上街头，欢庆胜利。

张　洁 / Zhang Jie

Beijing residents celebrate Beijing's winning bid to host the 2008 Olympic Games on July 13, 2001.

2008年8月8日，北京市故宫角楼，第29届奥运会在北京开幕，开幕式“大脚印”焰火越过故宫北门的瞬间。“大脚印”依次绽放在永定门、天安门、故宫，最后至鸟巢体育场上空，长达15公里的中轴线上。

文　闵 / Wen Min

A “footprint” in the sky for Beijing Olympic Games on August 8, 2008. Twenty-nine such “footprints” were fired into the sky for the opening of the Olympic Games.

2017年12月12日，北京市海淀区，颐和园十七孔桥，游人们争先恐后地拍摄“金光穿洞”奇观。

崔佰颖 / Cui Boying

Tourists are photographing the setting sun in the Summer Palace, Beijing, on December 12, 2017.

2018年5月19日，安徽省黄山市，游客排队上山，形成“龙盘黄山”的壮丽景观。 陈科云 / Chen Keyun

Tourists climb Mount Huangshan in East China's Anhui province on May 19, 2018.

2015年7月18日，四川省阿坝藏族羌族自治州，阿坝州若尔盖草原上的居民生活景象。

Life on the grassland in the Aba Tibetan and Qiang autonomous prefecture of Southwest China's Sichuan province, on July 18, 2015.

王达军 / Wang Dajun

2018年3月，湖南省湘潭县石潭镇，漫山遍野怒放的油菜花吸引游客登高望远，感受春天的气息。

Rape flowers blossom at Shitan town, Xiangtan county, Central China's Hunan province, in March, 2018.

解纪洪 / Xie Jihong

II

1983年4月，江苏省无锡市，南长街跨塘桥，上班高峰期，浩浩荡荡的自行车流堵得水泄不通。现在这里已成为步行街。

A bicycle jam at a bridge on Nanchang street, Wuxi city, East China's Jiangsu province, in April, 1983. Now it is a pedestrian-only street.

席建南 / Xi Jiannan

1982年3月6日，北京市南池子路口，公安部英模邵玉桥执勤过程中纠正一位闯红灯的骑车人。

刘英毅 / Liu Yingyi

Model police officer Shao Yuqiao politely stops a bicycle rider running a red light on March 6, 1982.

1981年，北京市，西四街头，交警执勤护送小学生过马路，孩子用敬礼的方式表达对警察叔叔的感谢。

A traffic police officer sends a girl across a zebra crossing in west Beijing in 1980. He did this everyday during peak hours.

张兆增 / Zhang Zhaozeng

1995年，河南省平顶山市，两位推着自行车赶集卖桑叉的农民。

张惠宾 / Zhang Huibin

Two men on their way to a market to sell wooden forks in Pingdingshan city, Central China's Henan province, in 1995.

1994年，河南省驻马店市泌阳县，农民在赶集路上艰辛跋涉。 周一渤 / Zhou Yibo

Wading through a river in Biyang county, Zhumadian city of Central China's Henan province, in 1994.

1994年，云南省福贡县，两岸之间没有桥梁，主要交通工具是溜索过江。

A man uses a zip line to cross the Nujiang River in Fugong county, Southwest China's Yunnan province, in 1994. There was no bridge at the time.

于志新 / Yu Zhixin

1984年，北京市建国门桥，两个男子赶着毛驴骑行在二环路上。

郭建设 / Guo Jianshe

Two men and their donkeys on Jianguomen street in Beijing in 1984.

1997年10月24日，安徽省合肥市，为综合治理市区交通秩序，志愿者在长江中路路口疏导交通。

A volunteer maintaining traffic order at Changjiang Zhonglu crossroad in Hefei city, East China's Anhui province, on October 24, 1997.

张　左 / Zhang Zuo

2017年4月26日，北京市朝阳区，共享单车遍布街头，管理员根据骑行者对自行车的需求进行调配。

王文澜 / Wang Wenlan

A warden is transporting shared bicycles to where they might be needed in Chaoyang district, Beijing, on April 26, 2017.

1982年，福建省福清市，自行车是人们日常的出行方式。

陈科云 / Chen Keyun

A pavement full of bicycles in Fuqing city, East China's Fujian province, in 1982.

1984年2月，北京东二环辅路，来自京郊农村的父子二人，顶风冒雪驮着自制的扫帚来市区送货。

A father and son take the brushes they have made to Beijing from their suburban village in February, 1984.

侯立印 / Hou Liyin

1994年2月，河北省涿州市，当地农民纷纷经商搞副业。

A rural villager selling feather dusters in Zhuozhou city, North China's Hebei province, in February, 1994,

张 屹 / Zhang Yi

1983年3月，上海市，安徽籍来沪的农民工在队长的带领下，推着独轮车，浩浩荡荡地在繁华的南京路上边走边看，进城务工。

Migrant workers from East China's Anhui province walk through Nanjing Road in Shanghai in March, 1983.

种　楠 / Zhong Nan

亨達利鐘表
不乱穿马路

2013年10月20日，广西壮族自治区南宁市凤岭村，女工在清运建筑垃圾。

李春龙 / Li Chunlong

A woman transporting construction rubbish at Fengling village, Nanning city of South China's Guangxi Zhuang autonomous region, on October 20, 2013.

1987年，北京市，长安街上，人力三轮车夫载着“圣诞老人”去外企发放节日礼物。 贾国荣 / Jia Guorong

Santa Clauses in tricycles on Chang'an Avenue, Beijing, in 1987.

1987年，北京市菜市口，工人师傅帮助顾客运送新买的“小天鹅”洗衣机。

刁立生 / Diao Lisheng

A woman gets help taking her newly-bought washing machine home in Beijing, 1987.

2012年6月8日，北京市内务部街，坐在电动车后座拥抱全家福照片的市民。 张居生 / Zhang Jusheng

Carrying a photo of a happy family on the back of an electric bicycle in Neiwubu Street, Beijing, on June 8, 2012.

2011年6月18日，湖北省武汉市，当地遭遇1998年以来最强暴雨袭击，汉口唐家墩路铁路涵洞下积水过深，一辆路过此地的婚车抛锚熄火。

石 一 / Shi Yi

A wedding car stranded in flood near a railway underpass in Wuhan, capital city of Central China's Hubei province, on June 18, 2011. The city was battered by heaviest rainstorm since 1998.

2004年10月，广西壮族自治区南宁市，一位工人在积水中抢修施工。

唐辉吉 / Tang Huiji

A worker trying to locate a manhole which was flooded in Nanning city, South China's Guangxi Zhuang autonomous region, in October, 2004 .

2016年1月26日，广西壮族自治区，春节临近，打工者为了更快到家过年，日夜兼程地骑摩托车带着亲人赶路。 赵 亢 / Zhao Kang

Migrant workers riding motorcycles home for Spring Festival in Guangxi Zhuang autonomous region on January 26, 2016.

1982年4月，河北省滦县，农民赶着毛驴穿梭在车水马龙的乡村土路上。

王文扬 / Wang Wenyang

A crowded road in Luanxian county, North China's Hebei province, in April, 1982.

2016年11月1日，北京市朝阳区东直门外，满载货物的快递配送车。

朱建辉 / Zhu Jianhui

A deliveryman checks his phone on Dongzhimenwai street of Chaoyang district in Beijing on November 1, 2016.

2017年3月30日，北京市东城区，送餐员身着统一制服，在南管公园门前集合待命，手机随时接单准备出发。

朱建辉 / Zhu Jianhui

Food delivery riders assemble at Nanguan Park in Dongcheng district, Beijing, on March 30, 2017.

2018年，北京市分司厅胡同，幼儿园门口排队接孩子的家长们。

吴 强 / Wu Qiang

Parents wait for their children outside a kindergarten in Beijing in 2018.

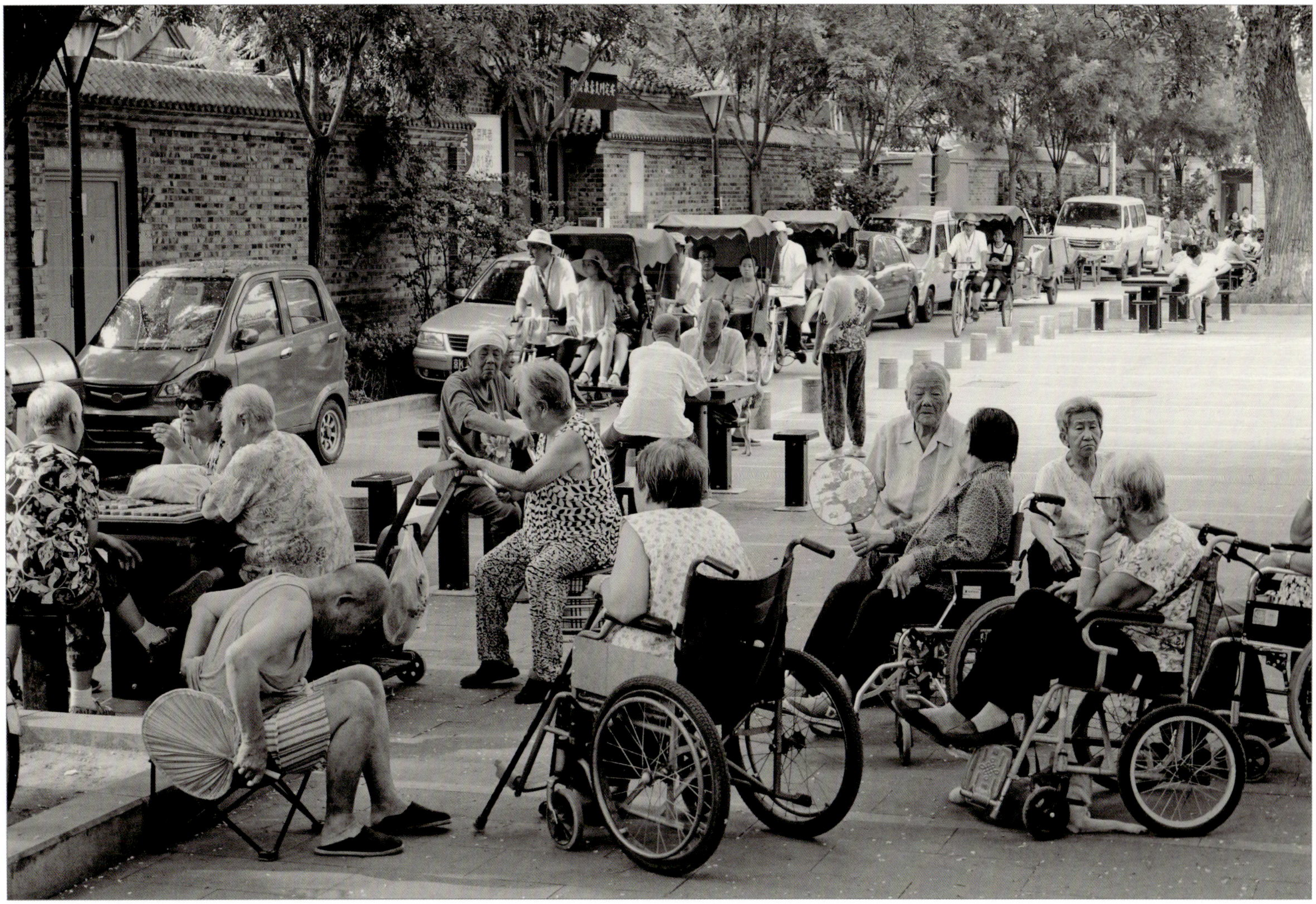

2017年8月30日，北京市东城区，炎热的夏季，在钟鼓楼广场休闲纳凉的老人们自娱自乐。

王 倪 / Wang Ni

Elderly residents at Drum Tower square, Dongcheng district in Beijing, on August 30, 2017.

2011年6月2日，河北省唐山市国际会展中心，越来越多的汽车厂商邀请模特为新车站台。

尹景利 / Yin Jingli

A model attracts people to check out a car at an auto exhibition at Tangshan International Exhibition Center in Tangshan city, North China's Hebei province, on June 2, 2011.

2015年，江苏省南京市江宁区，汤山风景区的游客各驾“宝马”上路。

杨慧宝 / Yang Huibao

A horse rider meets with a car driver in Tangshan scenic spot, Jiangning district, Nanjing city of East China's Jiangsu province, in 2015.

2000年12月18日，海南省海口市，海秀大道发生一起交通事故，涉事三人同时用手机向家人通报情况。

黄一鸣 / Huang Yiming

People involved in a traffic accident are on the phone in Haikou city, South China's Hainan province, on December 18, 2000.

2009年，山东省即墨市，新手司机上路，被困马路旁，热心人想办法解围。

李 舸 / Li Ge

Helping hands extended to a new driver in Jimo city of East China's Shandong province in 2009.

2007年3月11日，湖北省宜昌市，秭归滚装船码头，江苏盐城司机朱正飞带着妻儿跑运输。

李亚隆 / Li Yalong

A truck driver takes his wife and child with him while on the job at a port in Zigui county, Yichang city of Central China's Hubei province, on March 11, 2007.

1989年，北京市海淀区，大钟寺蔬菜批发市场由农民自发筹建，各种蔬菜销往全国20多个城市。 张兆增 / Zhang Zhaozeng

A scene at Beijing Dazhongsi vegetable wholesale market in 1989.

1989年春节后，重庆市，火车站售票处迎来客流高峰，乘客要排一夜的队才能购到票。

Queuing for a train ticket in Chongqing city, Southwest China's Sichuan province, in 1989. It was hard to buy a train ticket immediately after Spring Festival then.

袁学军 / Yuan Xuejun

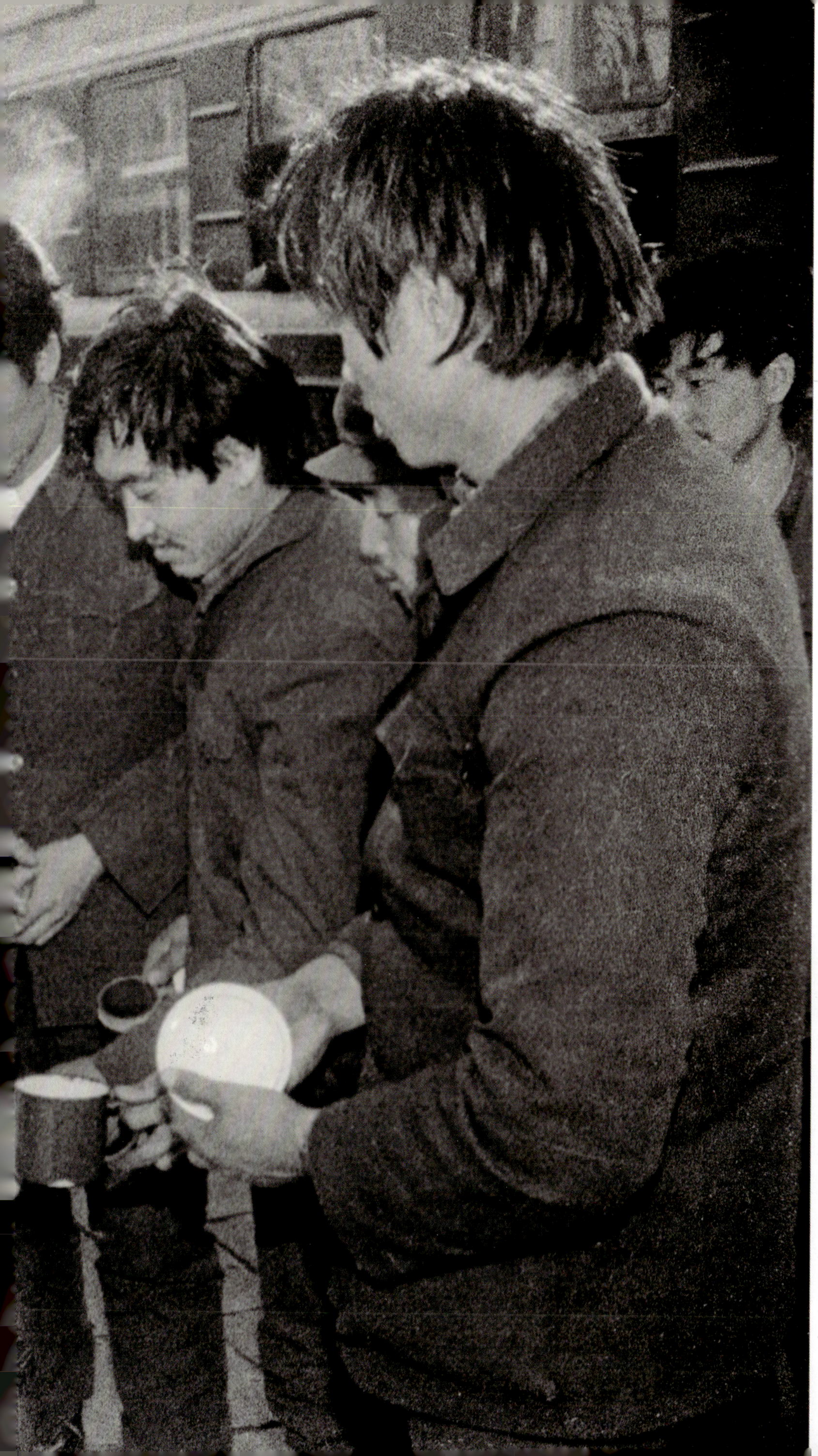

1982年春，内蒙古自治区通辽市，车站工作人员为过往旅客准备了热水。

Passengers get hot water at the station of Tongliao city, the Inner Mongolia autonomous region. when their train stops there in the early spring of 1982.

原瑞伦 / Yuan Ruilun

1982年夏，呼和浩特至北京的k90次列车上，列车员对前来补票的旅客应接不暇。

原瑞伦 / Yuan Ruilun

A train from Hohhot, capital of the Inner Mongolia automnomous region, to Beijing is packed with passengers in the summer of 1982.

2006年9月26日，由上海开往西藏的列车开通，一位乘务员与列车留影。

张 明 / Zhang Ming

Having a photo taken with the train from Shanghai to Lhasa, capital city of the Tibet autonomous region, on September 26, 2006.

2007年春节，吉林省临江市，松岭雪村的村民用牛爬犁将特产运输到火车站，前往市区赶集。

Boarding a train at Songling Station, Linjiang city of Northeast China's Jilin province, before Spring Festival in 2007. People were taking the train to the city fair to sell their specialties.

连承灏 / Lian Chenghao

2007年6月20日，四川省乐山市犍为县，嘉阳小火车是世界上唯一每天都在正常运营的蒸汽机车。

A driver with his small steam locomotive at Jianwei county, Southwest China's Sichuan province on June 20, 2007. The locomotive runs 19 kilometers from Minjiang station to Bajiaogou everyday. It is the only locomotive of its kind still in operation in the world.

程玉扬 / Cheng Yuyang

2005年8月13日，青藏高原建设工地，当地藏民与准备开往雪域高原的火车头合影。青藏铁路是通往西藏腹地的第一条铁路，也是世界上海拔最高、线路最长的高原铁路。

车刚 / Che Gang

Tibetans all smiles on the first locomotive to cross the world's highest pleteau on August 13, 2005. The railway to Lhasa in the Tibet autonomous region was officially opened on July 1, 2006.

1979年4月，北京市东城区，天坛公园首次举办天坛商品交易会，顾客抢购搪瓷保温杯。

徐建中 / Xu Jianzhong

People attending a commodity fair in the Temple of Heaven in Beijing in April, 1979.

1997年，辽宁省沈阳市，车主停车买货，亲自用秤称量验货。

A driver buys snacks without even leaving his car in Shenyang, Northeast China's Liaoning province in 1997.

严志刚 / Yan Zhigang

1978年，北京市火车站，春节前，旅客手提北京特产糕点返乡过年。

韩学章 / Han Xuezhang

Immediately before Spring Festival in 1978, passengers carrying boxes of Beijing snacks at Beijing Railway Station.

2015年4月29日，重庆市渝中区，挑夫们担着沉重的货物穿行在朝天门码头。

Porters known locally as 'bangbang' carry their loads through Chaotianmen Pier in Yuzhong district, Chongqing city, on April 29, 2015.

胡林庆 / Hu Linqing

1993年10月，北京市通州区，新华大街上的一名餐饮经营者沿街做广告招揽生意。

A restaurant owner advertises his food on Xinhua street in Tongzhou county, Beijing, in October, 1993.

康泰森 / Kang Taisen

砂鍋羊肚
砂鍋丸子
砂鍋吊子
砂鍋牛杂
砂鍋牛肚
砂鍋羊杂
砂鍋白菜
砂鍋牛肉

1980年，北京市西单菜市场，市场不仅有活鸡出售，还新增“代客宰鸡”项目。

方学辉 / Fang Xuehui

Chicken being sold in Xidan food market, Beijing, in 1980.

1987年，广东省广州市，物资丰富的自由市场，市民购买鸡鸭鱼肉。

翁乃强 / Weng Naiqiang

A freemarket in Guangzhou city, South China's Guangdong province in 1987.

2006年4月8日，广西壮族自治区鹿寨县寨沙镇，农民将鸭群赶过街市，到水塘河沟放养。

蒋建雄 / Jiang Jianxiong

A farmer with his ducks on the street at Zhaisha town, Luzhai county, South China's Guangxi Zhuang autonomous region, on April 8, 2006.

2002年，四川省南部县蹍垭乡，摩托车超载，在上坡路时翻了车。

杨 麾 / Yang Hui

A motorcycle topples over as it is overloaded with ducks on an unpaved road in Nianya town, Nanbu county, Southwest China's Sichuan province, in 2002.

1994年，河南省平顶山市，生猪交易市场繁忙兴旺。

A pig market in Pingdingshan city, Central China's Henan province, in 1994.

张惠宾 / Zhang Huibin

1987年，广东省广州市，河沿早市上贩卖自产蔬菜的菜农们。

A morning vegetable market in Guangzhou city, South China's Guangdong province, in 1987.

翁乃强 / Weng Naiqiang

1997年10月，北京市东城区，东华门早市，市民们选购新鲜蔬菜。

A morning market by the East Gate of the Forbidden City in Beijing in October, 1997.

张锁安 / Zhang Suoan

2010年8月29日，湖北省郧县，南水北调中最大规模的水上移民搬迁。

赵 亢 / Zhao Kang

Local residents in Yunxian county, Central China's Hubei province, being relocated for the project to divert water from South China to North China on August 29, 2010.

2006年5月，广东省珠海市，每天清晨，数百位挑着各色鲜花担子的花农齐聚码头，拱北海关关员依规章快速核定后，船只即刻通关起航，驶向澳门特别行政区，直销鲜花。

邓 维 / Deng Wei

Flower growers gather at Gongbei Customs in Zhuhai city, South China's Guangdong province, to take the ferry to Macao to sell their flowers in May, 2006.

2010年4月，山东省寿光市，蔬菜博览园采用高科技无土栽培技术，改变了农业的传统种植。

李德林 / Li Delin

A vegetable expo shows how vegetables can be grown without soil in Shouguang city, East China's Shandong province, in April, 2010.

2014年8月11日，四川省彭州市，兰花交易市场。每年春秋两季是兰花分种与上市交易的好时节。 刘晓冀 / Liu Xiaoji

Buyers inspect Orchids at a flower fair in Pengzhou city, Southwest China's Sichuan province, on August 11, 2014.

1981年，山东省乳山市，妇女们在农村供销社挑选布料。

侯贺良 / Hou Heliang

Villagers selecting cloth at a local shop in Rushan city, East China's Shandong province, in 1981.

2016年11月18日，四川省凉山彝族自治州，赶集的妇女在挑选布料。

陈怡成 / Chen Yicheng

Women choosing colorful sheets in Liangshan Yi Minority autonomous prefecture, Southwest China's Sichuan province, on November 18, 2016.

1994年，辽宁省沈阳市，五爱市场是东北亚经济圈和环渤海经济圈最大的流转型轻工产品交易中心。

邓 维 / Deng Wei

A scene of Wuai Fair in Shenyang city, Northeast China's Liaoning province, in 1994. The fair was typical in the early years of reform and opening up. It is now a trade center of light indutrial commodities.

黄陂青年楚剧团
2

2017年10月24日，北京市延庆区，来自河北邢台的农民工在宿舍里，睡前上网玩手机。

李春龙 / Li Chunlong

Migrant workers pass the time on their smartphones in their dorm in Yanqing district, Beijing, on October 24, 2017.

2003年5月21日，广东省广州市番禺区，一家韩资企业的女工宿舍。她们来自四川、湖南、贵州等地，从事着流水线上的插件工作。

Female migrant workers in their dormitory in Panyu district, Guangzhou city, South China's Guangdong province, on May 21, 2003.

李洁军 / Li Jiejun

2005年6月13日，四川省富顺县赵化镇，朴实健硕的送煤工用人力车为居民送蜂窝煤。

A worker unloading honeycomb briquettes from his cart at Zhaohua town, Fushun county of Southwest China's Sichuan province on June 13, 2005.

程玉扬 / Cheng Yuyang

2004年7月17日，湖北省宜昌市，三峡工程右岸工地的农民工。

李亚隆 / Li Yalong

Migrant workers having a meal at the construction site of the Three Gorges Dam on July 17, 2004.

1985年，广东省深圳市，改革开放吸引了大批外来务工青年，集体宿舍成为了她们暂时的落脚点。

Dormitories for female migrant workers in Shenzhen, South China's Guangdong province, in 1985.

朱宪民 / Zhu Xianmin

1992年8月，福建省南安市，雪峰华侨农场与港商联办针织厂，女工们在生产线上繁忙劳作。 祝敏松 / Zhu Minsong

Migrant workers at work in a textile plant in Nan'an city, East China's Fujian province, in August, 1992.

2006年，北京市，外地来京务工的农民工携带行李，兴高采烈地来到天安门广场参观。

周明星 / Zhou Mingxing

Migrant workers at Tian'anmen Square in Beijing in 2006.

1993年，北京天安门广场，随着中国新一轮经济大潮的兴起，大量的农民工离开故土，走进大都市，寻找工作机会。

袁学军 / Yuan Xuejun

Migrant workers at Tian'anmen Square in Beijing In 1993. Villagers come to big cities such as Beijing looking for jobs.

2013年5月23日，四川省泸州市叙永县，两户农民用自制滑竿把两台冰箱抬回家。

曾 朗 / Zeng Lang

Villagers transporting refrigrators home along mountain paths in Xuyong county, Luzhou city of Southwest China's Sichuan province, on May 23, 2013.

1982年，云南省大理市，经济发展后，当地人背着用大理石做的家具到自由市场去出售。　王　苗 / Wang Miao

Taking marble tea tables to market in Dali city, Southwest China's Yunnan province, in 1982.

2017年4月8日，福建省福鼎市，茶市现场气氛火爆，来往人群构成流动的茶田。

People attend a tea fair in Fuding city, East China's Fujian province, on April 8, 2017.

姜 建 / Jiang Jian

1986年，浙江省杭州市，千岛湖捕捞队员们在队长统一指挥下合力拉起巨型渔网，狂舞的鱼群跃出水面。

A harvest of fish at Qiandao Lake in Hangzhou, capital city of East China's Zhejiang province, in 1986.

吴宗其 / Wu Zongqi

III

灯号
11030308
i ♥ family

2015年9月8日，上海外滩，来自东北的游客拉着手提行李箱在景点合影留念。

Tourists take a photo on the Bund in Shanghai on September 8, 2015.

沈敏觉 / Shen Minjue

励

1984年，北京市门头沟区大台街道，千军台村、庄户村每年正月十五、十六举行古幡盛会。据明代典籍记载从明初到明末的二百年间，幡旗之队列，乐曲之演奏最为繁盛。一是幡、二是乐，既有旌旗招展，又有乐曲相伴，场面庄严肃穆，情景交融，盛况空前。

An ancient flag fair is staged at Qianjuntai village, Mentougou district, Beijing, on February 16, 1984. This fair is an intangible cultural heritage.

朱宪民 / Zhu Xianmin

2001年，北京故宫，几位来自山东省滨州市堡集市敬老院的老人平生第一次来到故宫，十分欣喜，左顾右盼。 李 楠 / Li Nan

Elderly women with bound feet in the Forbidden City in 2001. From a nursing home in Binzhou city, East China's Shandong province, they could not imagine that they would visit Beijing in their lifetime. But they did.

1985年，北京天安门广场，来自边远地区的游客第一次来到首都，难掩内心喜悦。 侯贺良 / Hou Heliang

A tourist at Tian'anmen Squares shows her excitement on visiting Beijing for the first time in 1985.

1995年，陕西省宜川县，淳朴、善良、好客的陕北老乡们在大树下休闲纳凉。 刘 雷 / Liu Lei

Elderly villagers taking shelter under a big tree in northern Shaanxi province in 1995.

1981年，辽宁省新宾满族自治县，严冬外出的人们躲到树洞中避寒等车，天然的树洞成了临时的交通驿站。

A talk in an old tree at Xinbin Man autonomous county, Northeast China's Liaoning province, in 1981.

王玉文 / Wang Yuwen

1986年12月，陕西省榆林市横山区响水镇，村民们冒雪迎接新娘，大雪纷飞给喜庆的日子增添了别致的氛围。

A wedding in the snow in northern Shaanxi province in 1986.

潘　科 / Pan Ke

1990年4月，陕西省宝鸡县凤阁岭乡，乡村摄影师在简易的幕布的图案前为村民留影。

石宝琇 / Shi Baoxiu

Local residents have their photo taken in Fenggeling town, Baoji county of Northwest China's Shaanxi province, in April, 1990.

1981年，陕西省西安市大雁塔，几个卡车司机先后在简易搭成的背景中拍摄乘飞机照。

李英杰 / Li Yingjie

Truck drivers have a photo taken so they appear to be flying plane in Xi'an, capital city of Northwest China's Shaanxi province, in 1981.

2009年2月8日，甘肃省临夏回族自治州，摄影团队为当地保安族拍照，该团队历时一年完成大型文献画册《和谐中华》，详尽记录了我国五十六个民族的文化习俗。

崔新华 / Cui Xinhua

A photographer takes photos of people of the Bonan ethic group in Linxia Hui autonomous prefecture, West China's Gansu province, on February 8, 2009. It takes the team a year to finish an album titled Harmonious China, recording the cultures of all ethnic groups in the country.

2011年，北京市朝阳区东坝乡七棵树，京城首家水下摄影工作室，摄影师在为顾客拍摄水下写真集。水下写真受到越来越多的时尚青年追捧，使“旱鸭子”摇身变成“美人鱼”。

孙 妍 / Sun Yan

Having a photo taken underwater at a underwater photo studio in Chaoyang district, Beijing, in 2011. It was the first photo studio of its kind in Beijing then.

1996年8月1日，北京百鸟园正式接待游客，园区占地100亩，饲养80余个种类、2500只鸟。来自乌干达的国鸟——冠鹤，用其特殊的方式欢迎游客。

A bird startles a young woman at Paradise for Birds in Beijing on August 1, 1996. The park has 2,500 birds of different kinds.

陆中秋 / Lu Zhongqiu

2008年10月19日，北京市顺义区，游人在顺义马术俱乐部观赏马匹。

A young girl wants to pat a horse at an equestrian club at Shunyi district, Beijing, on October 19, 2008.

王希宝 / Wang Xibao

1980年，山西省左云县上张家坟村，富民政策让穷村走上致富路，村里买回第一台黑白电视机，全村村民高兴地在一起看电视。

A scene of villagers watching the only black and white television in Shangzhangjiafen village, Zuoyun county of North China's Shanxi province, in 1980.

王 悦 / Wang Yue

2014年1月24日，四川省绵阳市三台县，逢年过节，老街上的住户都会准备一桌丰盛的“百家宴”，宴请远道而来的宾客。

龙厚德 / Long Houde

A feast for all on January 24, 2014 in Santai county, Mianyang city of Southwest China's Sichuan province. Every family placed dishes they had cooked outside their home for locals and guests to enjoy.

1991年4月，江苏省泰州市溱潼镇，国内唯一保存最完整、最具原生态特质的水上庙会。

欧阳鹤 / Ouyang He

A temple fair on water in Qintong town, Taizhou city of East China's Jiangsu province in April, 1991. It was then the only fair held on water nationwide.

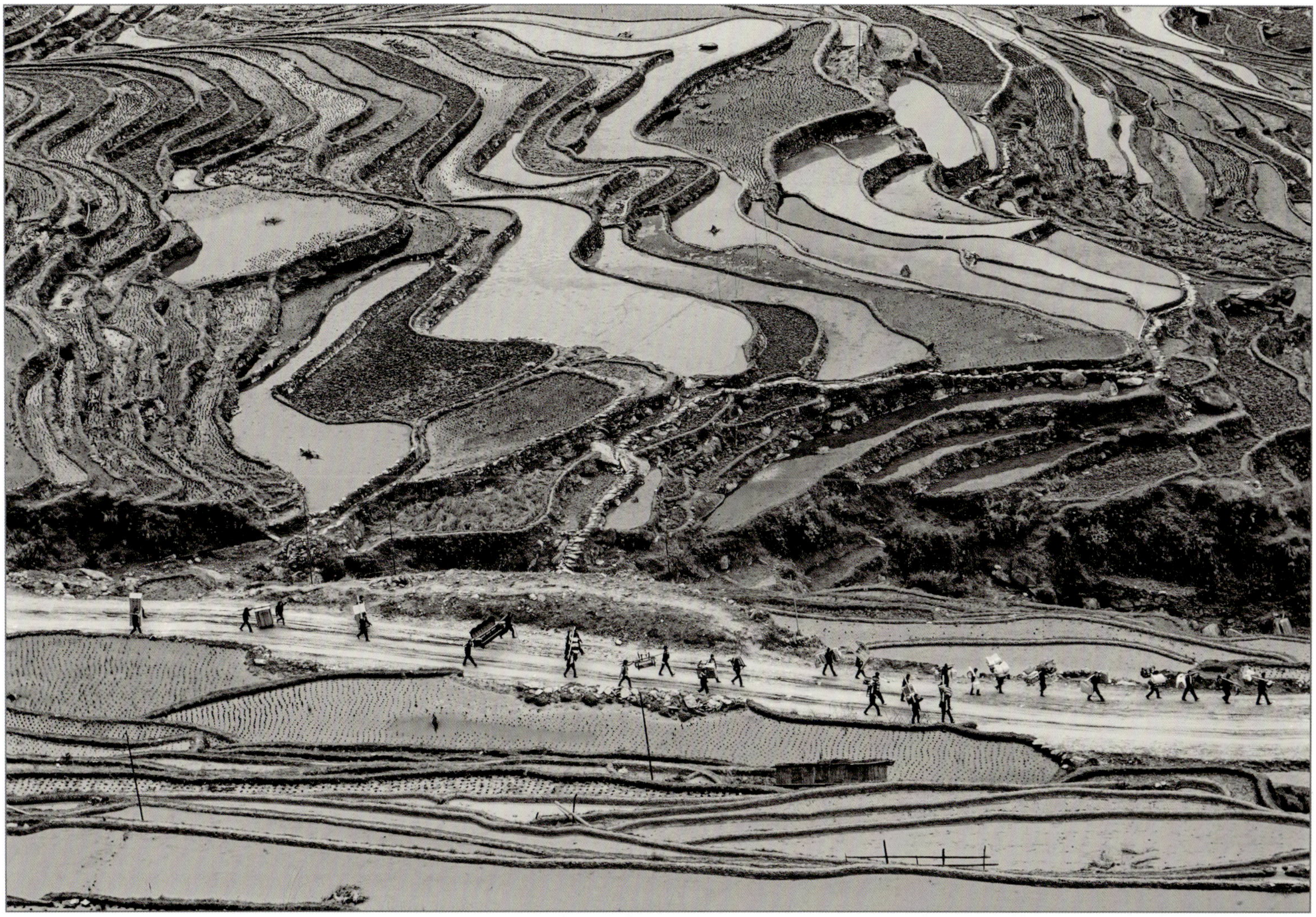

2012年4月9日，贵州省黔东南县加榜乡，侗族迎亲队伍浩浩荡荡，蜿蜒的山路，层层的梯田，呈现一幅人与自然和谐共存的画卷。

邱太建 / Qiu Taijian

A glimpse of terraced fields in Jiabang town, Dongnan county of Southwest China's Guizhou province, on April 9, 2012.

1984年，浙江省淳安县，
当地农村掀起过一阵子烫
卷发的时髦浪潮。

Women getting their hair done at a hairdressers in Chun'an county, East China's Zhejiang province, in 1984.

吴宗其 / Wu Zongqi

1994年10月1日，北京市西城区，象牙胡同里追赶时尚潮流的人们。

王文扬 / Wang Wenyang

A glimpse of life in a lane in Beijing on October 1, 1994.

1992年12月，上海市，香港著名美容大师郑明明在华联商厦的柜台推销增白化妆品。

A Hong Kong beautician promoting cosmetics in a shopping center in Shanghai in December, 1992.

于文国 / Yu Wenguo

1986年，北京市云居胡同，新婚夫妇与新郎父母在家门口合影。 贾 勇 / Jia Yong

Newly weds with one set of parents at Yunju Lane, Beijing, in 1986.

1980年4月，北京市东城区，共青团北京市委员会在劳动人民文化宫为五十对新人举办集体婚礼。 侯立印 / Hou Liyin

A group wedding for 50 couples at the Workers' Cultural Palace in Beijing in April, 1980.

1982年，山东省日照市，村民们祝贺一对新人喜结连理。

侯贺良 / Hou Heliang

A rural couple enjoy their wedding in Rizhao city, East China's Shandong province, in 1982.

2013年，北京市故宫角楼，一对恋人幸福地拍摄婚纱照。 郭培和 / Guo Peihe

A couple have photos taken for their wedding outside the Forbidden Palace in Beijing in 2013.

2018年5月12日，香港特别行政区，太古城商场里行色匆匆的人群。

People in Cityplaza, Hong Kong, on May 12, 2018.

姜 建 / Jiang Jian

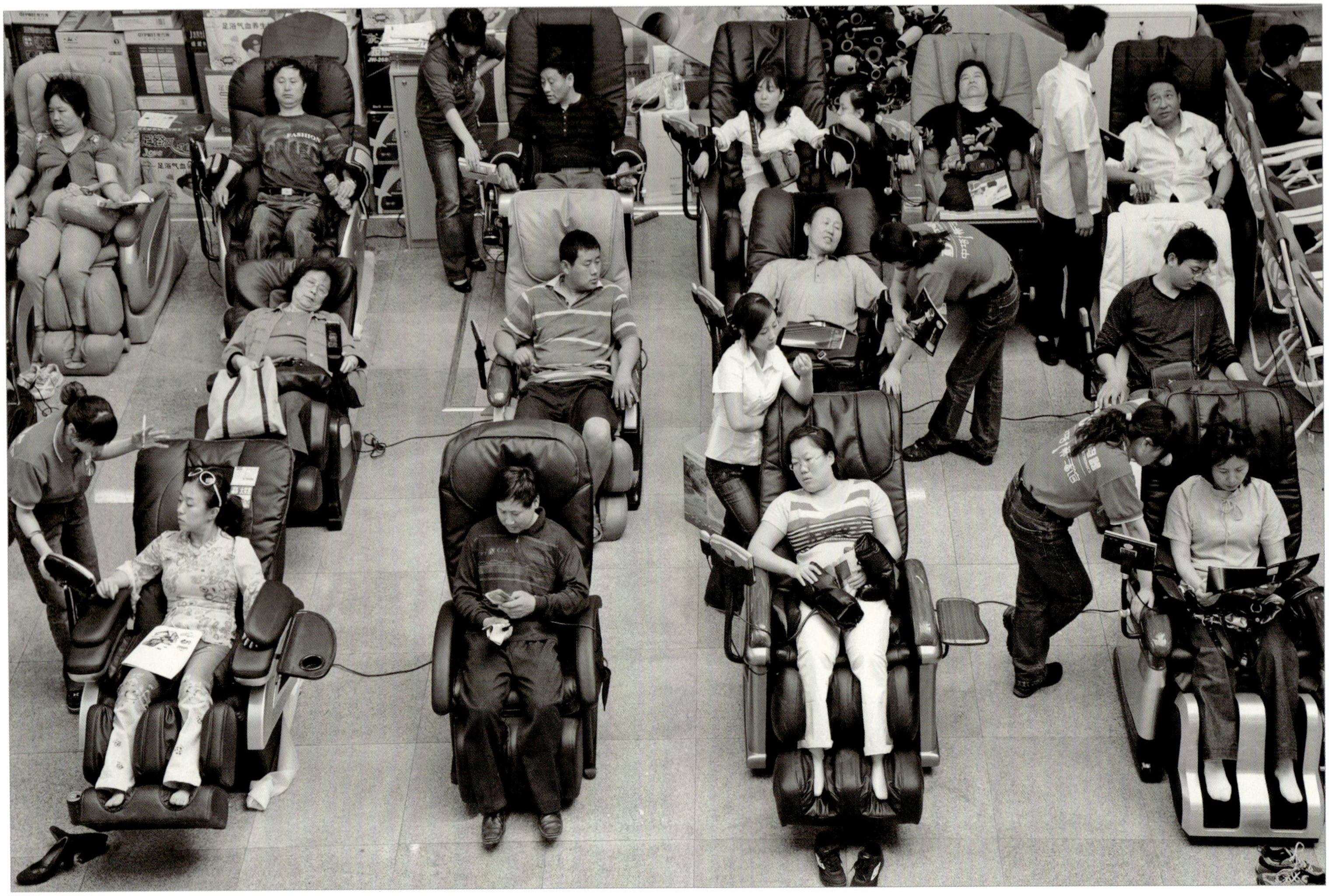

2009年5月3日，北京市海淀区，中央电视塔附近的大中电器商城，节日里，商场专门为顾客提供了休息按摩区。

黄冠海 / Huang Guanhai

Electric massage chairs are being promoted at an electric appliances market in Beijing on May 3, 2009.

2018年4月23日，香港特别行政区铜锣湾，几位自由行游客满载而归。

姜 建 / Jiang Jian

Tourists in Hong Kong on April 23, 2018.

JACK

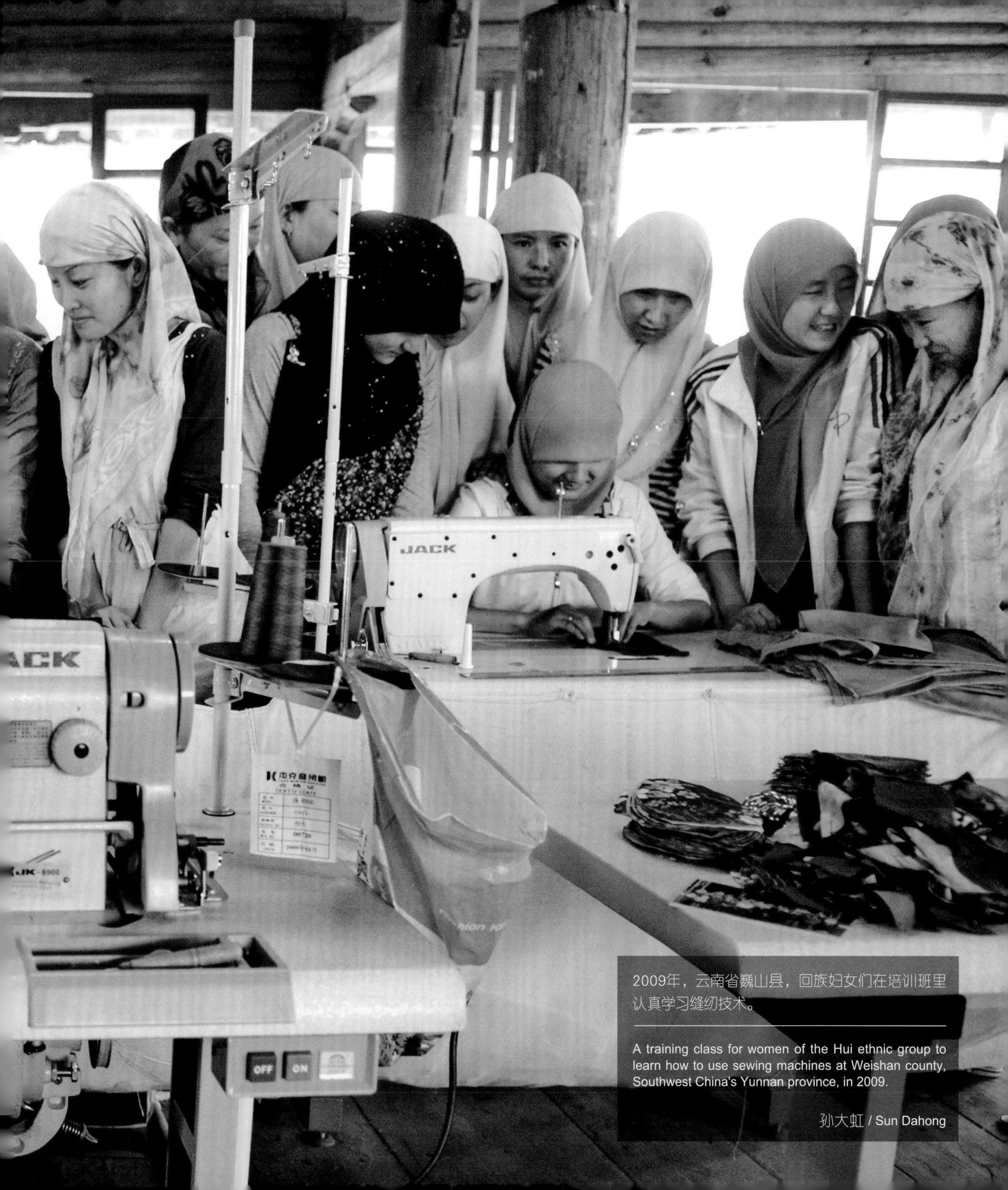

2009年，云南省巍山县，回族妇女们在培训班里认真学习缝纫技术。

A training class for women of the Hui ethnic group to learn how to use sewing machines at Weishan county, Southwest China's Yunnan province, in 2009.

孙大虹 / Sun Dahong

2017年10月14日，广西壮族自治区三江县林溪镇程阳寨，当地的侗族百家宴颇具民俗风味。侗族人用最高规格的接待，让宾客们感受了百人就餐的盛大家宴。

刘丽华 / Liu Lihua

A long table banquet with participation of all local families at Chengyangzhai village, Linxi town of Sanjiang county in South China's Guangxi Zhuang autonomous region, on October 14, 2017.

2000年3月13日，云南省大姚县昙华乡彝族传统节日插花节，人们身着节日盛装在昙华山中欢聚，举行祭花活动。

刘世昭 / Liu Shizhao

At the flower festival of Yi ethnic group in Tanhua town, Dayao county of Southwest China's Yunnan province, on March 13, 2000.

2011年3月5日，湖南省凤凰县禾库镇，同车隔代的苗族女性。

康泰森 / Kang Taisen

A girl of the Miao ethnic group wearing colorful clothes stands out among the elderly women wearing traditional clothes in Heku town, Fenghuang county, Central China's Hunan province, on March 5, 2011.

2016年10月，贵州省松桃县，苗寨婚礼上的录像师和围观的乡亲们。 奚耀华 / Xi Yaohua

Shooting a wedding at a village of the Miao ethnic group in Songtao county, Southwest China's Guizhou province in October, 2016.

2016年7月23日，四川省凉山彝族自治州布拖县，改革开放后的大凉山彝族"火把节"期间，彝族女性精心打扮，在大街上巡游，展示民族文化的魅力。

Women of the Yi ethnic group in their traditional costumes and decorations parading on a street in Butuo county, Liangshan Yi autonomous prefecture, Southwest China's Sichuan province, on July 23, 2016, during the local torch festival.

周本意 / Zhou Benyi

2010年，内蒙古自治区鄂尔多斯市伊金霍洛苏木乡，祭祀活动中，牧民开展骆驼球比赛活动。

王卫光 / Wang Weiguang

Herdsmen playing polo on camels in Yijinhuoluosumu town, Erdos city, the Inner Mongolia autonomous region, in 2010.

2011年7月，内蒙古自治区锡林郭勒盟，几位少年选手在草原上赛马。 李德林 / Li Delin

Children having fun in a horse race in Xilin Gol League, the Inner Mongolia autonomous region, in July, 2011.

2016年，内蒙古自治区锡林浩特市，人与马在草原上进行一场较量。 黄松辉/ Huang Songhui

Men round up colts in Xilinhot grassland in the Inner Mongolia autonomous region in 2016.

2017年10月23日，内蒙古自治区通辽市奈曼旗，蒙古族传统婚礼习俗具有独特的民族特色，隆重的婚礼场面显得格外喜庆。 袁 奕 / Yuan Yi

A bride on her way to her wedding at Naiman Banner in the Inner Mongolia autonomous region on October 23, 2017.

2014年8月28日，内蒙古自治区达茂草原，小摔跤手哈林与爷爷在草地上练习。

贾 婷 / Jia Ting

A boy practises wrestling in front of his grandfather in Damao Grassland in the Inner Mongolia autonomous region on August 28, 2014.

2008年7月30日，内蒙古自治区呼伦贝尔草原，牧民正在挤牛奶，淳朴的一家人享受着醇美的劳动成果。

巴义尔 / Ba Yier

Herdswoman milks her cow in Hulunbuir, the Inner Mongolia autonomous region, on July 30, 2008.

2003年2月，四川省阿坝藏族羌族自治州，一位藏族小女孩在雪地里放牛。

A Tibetan girl leads a yak through the snow in the Aba Tibetan and Qiang autonomous prefecture, Southwest China's Sichuan province, in February, 2003.

冯凯文 / Feng Kaiwen

1989年3月15日，云南省大姚县，彝族群众在传统节日里引吭高歌，互动对唱，用录音机录制自己喜爱的山歌。

A glimpse of a traditional festival at Dayao county, Southwest China's Yunnan province, on March 15, 1989.

王　苗 / Wang Miao

2007年8月14日，青海省玉树藏族自治州，一个女孩在草原上摊牛粪。

冯凯文 / Feng Kaiwen

A girl spreads yak dung in the Yushu Tibet autonomous prefecture, West China's Qinghai province, on August 14, 2007.

2009年10月，四川省壤塘县，一户藏民建新居，楼梯间坐满了喜气洋洋的藏族村民。

冯凯文 / Feng Kaiwen

Local villagers celebrate the building of a new house for a family in Rangtang county of Sichuan province, in October, 2009.

GUCCI

2016年3月，四川省阿坝县四哇乡，大家在齐心合力地建设家园。

A house is under construction in Siwa town, Aba county, Southwest China's Sichuan province, in March, 2016.

李 刚 / Li Gang

2003年9月28日，四川省松潘县，九寨黄龙机场开幕典礼上，阿坝藏族羌族自治州的各民族来宾用传统的仪式在祈祷吉祥、安康。

刘世昭 / Liu Shizhao

Local Tibetans and residents of the Qiang ethnic group at the ceremony to inaugurate Huanglong Airport in Songpan county, Southwest China's Sichuan province, on September 28, 2003.

2005年6月30日，西藏自治区拉萨市，雪顿节期间，哲蚌寺举行展佛活动。展佛节当天，拉萨城数十万信教群众和游客早早地涌上哲蚌寺所在的山上瞻仰朝拜。

车刚 / Che Gang

Thousands of Buddhism believers and tourists pay tribute to the Buddha at Drepung Monastery, Lhasa, the Tibet autonomous region, on June 30, 2005.

2005年2月，甘肃省甘南藏族自治州碌曲县郎木寺镇，零下二十八度的低温天气，祈祷仪式上的藏族僧侣们。

李景琳 / Li Jinglin

A burial ceremony at Langmusi town, Luqu county, Gannan Tibet autonomous prefecture of West China's Gansu province, in February, 2005.

2005年，甘肃省甘南藏族自治州，身着民族服饰的藏族群众在赶往拉卜楞寺途中小歇。

李小可 / Li Xiaoke

On a pilgrimage to Labrang Lamasery in Gannan Tibet autonomous prefecture of West China's Gansu province in 2005.

2017年7月9日，甘肃省甘南藏族自治州玛曲县，煮酥油茶非常讲究茶和奶的配比，是藏族妇女必备的生活技能。

刘秀军 / Liu Xiujun

A Tibetan woman makes buttered tea in Maqu county, Gannan Tibet autonomous prefecture, Gansu province, on July 9, 2017.

2016年，西藏自治区阿里地区普兰县，身着华丽的藏族“孔雀”服饰的妇女们。

滕 俊 / Teng Jun

Tibetan women in traditional dress in Pulan county, Ali prefecture, the Tibet autonomous region, in 2016.

2016年10月，新疆维吾尔自治区喀什市，牲口交易市场，小羊扎在老主人怀里恋恋不舍。

韩文杰 / Han Wenjie

A cattle fair in Kashgar city, the Xinjiang Uygur autonomous region, in October 2016.

2012年12月14日，新疆维吾尔自治区富蕴县，哈萨克族牧民骑着马，抱着熟睡的孩子，带着骆驼，拖着转场用的全部家当，从秋牧场向冬牧场进发。

钱 捍 / Qian Han

A Kazak on his way to a winter pasture in Fuyun county, the Xinjiang Uygur autonomous region, on December 14, 2012.

2013年9月19日，新疆维吾尔自治区和田市，妇女们在大巴扎上购物，琳琅满目的各色面料让人眼花缭乱。

At a bazaar in Hotan city, the Xinjiang Uygur autonomous region, on September 19, 2013.

束黎明 / Shu Liming

2016年6月13日，新疆维吾尔自治区乌鲁木齐市利民巷，各族民众聚在一起共度“斋月”。

A street banquet at Limin Lane, Urumqi, capital city of the Xinjiang Uygur autonomous region, on June 13, 2016.

束黎明 / Shu Liming

2007年，新疆维吾尔自治区喀什市莎车县，十二木卡姆艺术节，几位老汉功力不减当年。

黄松辉/ Huang Songhui

Elderly Uygurs singing at an local arts festival in Yarkant county in the Xinjiang Uygur autonomous region in 2007.

2006年，新疆维吾尔自治区和田市，赶巴扎回来的维族老乡在行路期间开怀畅聊。

Elderly Uygurs happy on their return from a bazaar in Hotan city in the Xinjiang Uygur autonomous region in 2006.

黄松辉/ Huang Songhui

2007年，新疆维吾尔自治区塔什库尔干，塔吉克族一家人盘坐在一起吃午餐。

A Tajik family at lunch in Tashikurgan in the Xinjiang Uygur autonomous region in 2007.

黄松辉 / Huang Songhui

2015年7月7日，北京市朝阳区，在三里屯街头卖气球的小贩们。
三里屯已经成为了时尚的代名词。

吕小中 / Lyu Xiaozhong

Pedlars selling balloons in Sanlitun street, Beijing, on July 7, 2015.

2016年，北京市东城区，南锣鼓巷一家卖国产护肤品的商店，橱窗里琳琅满目的商品与古色古香的胡同背景互相映衬。

张 威 / Zhang Wei

A look through the window of a shop selling traditional cosmetics in Nanluoguxiang lane, Beijing, in 2016.

1997年，北京市朝阳区，可口可乐公司把巨大的霓虹灯广告，摆到了建国门外金桥大厦的楼顶。 胡金喜 / Hu Jinxi

A Coca Cola advertisement above Jinqiao Tower at Jianguomenwai Street in Beijing in 1997.

1981年，北京天安门金水桥，大碗茶摊上，东道主以茶会友，招待外国游客。

王文波 / Wang Wenbo

Having a bowl of tea in front Golden Water Bridge at the foot of Tian'anmen Tower in Beijing in 1981.

2004年9月19日，上海市，旅游节开幕式上，一位外国友人与市民共舞。 沈敏觉 / Shen Minjue

At the opening ceremony of Shanghai Tourism Festival on September 19, 2004.

1985年，陕西省西安市新城区，来往民众在解放路围观外宾。随着改革开放，越来越多的国际友人到中国旅行。

潘 科 / Pan Ke

Foreigners under the gaze of Chinese in Xincheng district, Xi'an, capital of Northwest China's Shaanxi province, in 1985.

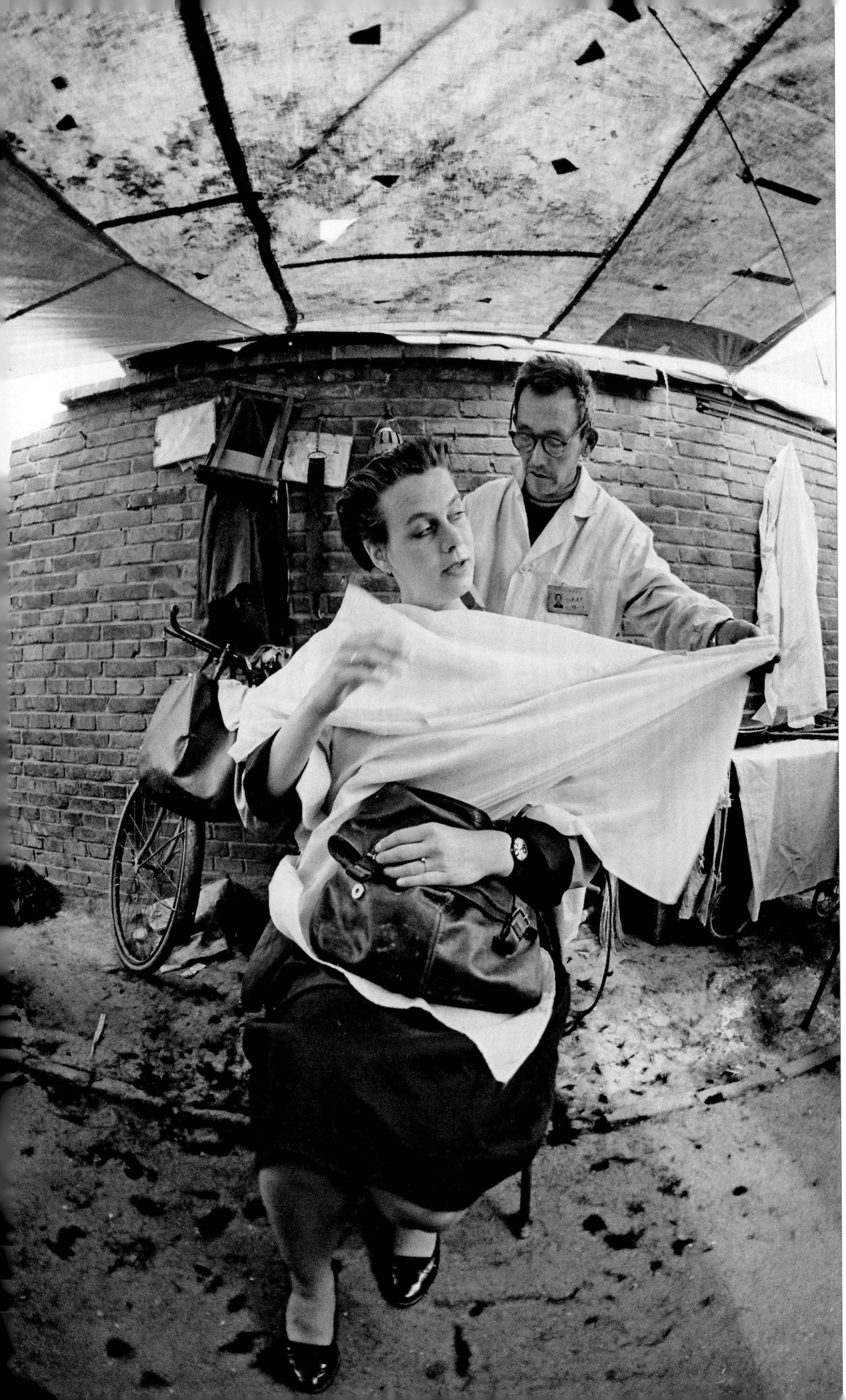

1988年9月，北京市西城区，官园花鸟鱼虫市场内的理发摊，北京大学荷兰籍女留学生请理发师给她剪个短发。

A Dutch woman having a haircut at a fair in Beijing in September 1988.

王文泉 / Wang Wenquan

1992年，北京市天坛公园，国际知名品牌路易·威登新闻发布会上，用LV皮具搭起法国埃菲尔铁塔的造型进行展示，古色古香的民族服装与西方时尚相融合。

A photoshoot for the release of new Louis Vuitton bags and cases at the Temple of Heaven in 1992.

王文澜 / Wang Wenlan

2015年7月，江苏省苏州市，苏州大学的外国留学生练习中国书法。

唐苏民 / Tang Sumin

Practising Chinese calligraphy and painting at Suzhou University, East China's Jiangsu province, in July, 2015.

2007年6月，上海市复兴公园，居住在上海的外国居民举行一年一度的“泼水节”。

徐正魁 / Xu Zhengkui

Foreign residents in Shanghai having a water fight in Fuxing Park in June, 2007. It is an annual activity.

2006年，陕西省华县魏家塬村，来自法国的摄制组为皮影老艺人录像并录音。

张 韬 / Zhang Tao

A documenatry team from France shoot a video of elderly artists performing a shadow play in Weijiayuan village of Huaxian county, Northwest China's Shaanxi province, in 2006.

2013年12月31日，澳门特别行政区陆军俱乐部，在澳门出生、生活的葡萄牙人吹奏小号迎新年。 郭敬文 / Guo Jingwen

An evening party to welcome the coming New Year at a club in Macao on December 31, 2013.

2001年6月23日，北京故宫午门前，世界三大男高音歌唱家（左起）普拉西多·多明戈、何塞·卡雷拉斯、鲁契亚诺·帕瓦罗蒂为中国观众举办演唱会。

José Plácido Domingo Embi (first from left), José Carreras (center) and Luciano Pavarotti perform together in front of the Forbidden City in Beijing on June 23, 2001.

卢北峰 / Lu Beifeng

2018年8月17日，浙江省宁波市月湖公园，一位比利时的游客与当地的老人通过手机翻译软件聊天，有朋自远方来不亦乐乎。

A Belgian tourist chats with a Chinese man with the help of smartphone interpretation software at Moon Lake Park, Ningbo city of East China's Zhejiang province, on August 17, 2018.

王文澜 / Wang Wenlan

2017年9月23日，四川省成都市人民公园，当地文化旅游机构的工作人员以幽默诙谐的“展言子”向中外游客介绍川蜀文化。“展言子”是一种与北方“侃大山”类似的语言艺术形式。

陈 锦 / Chen Jin

A local woman introduces Sichuan culture to tourists in Renmin Park in Chengdu, capital of Southwest China's Sichuan province, on September 23, 2017.

1979年，北京天坛，游客排长队一饱耳福，感受回音壁的魅力。

Listening to echoes at the Echo Wall of the Temple of Heaven in Beijing in 1979.

王文波 / Wang Wenbo

2014年9月16日，河北省唐山市，老干部活动中心离退休职工排演的皮影舞《俏夕阳》登上央视春晚的舞台后，不少外国人慕名而来学习皮影舞。

Retirees in Tangshan city, North China's Hebei province, rehearse their well-known dance Lively Eldly Women, which immitates shadow play figures, on September 16, 2014,

成贵民 / Cheng Guimin

IV

2011年，云南省宣威市保山镇，学校操场上，孩子们整齐列队，老师逐一检查学生们在小黑板上写的作业。

朱宪民

Pupils hold small blackboards in front of them at a primary school in Yunnan province, in 2011.

Zhu Xianmin

2013年12月23日，北京市，史家胡同小学的孩子们在中国国家博物馆，参观纪念毛泽东诞辰120周年展览。

Students from Shijiahutong Primary School visit an exhibition in memory of Mao Zedong's birthday at National Musuem of China on December 23, 2013.

姜 东 / Jiang Dong

1994年，辽宁省沈阳市于洪区汪家小学门前，几位小学生在学雷锋活动月中，开展助人为乐服务。

梁达明 / Liang Daming

Primary school pupils happy to be good Samaritans in Yuhong district, Shenyang city of Northeast China's Liaoning province, in 1994.

1982年春天，北京市西城区，全国展开“五讲四美”爱国运动，北长街小学把北海团城一带作为“红领巾卫生街”。

Primary school pupils clean a route board at a bus stop in Beijing in the spring of 1982.

许　林 / Xu Lin

1992年3月10日，河南省原阳县李庄村，小学生点着蜡烛上晚自习。

陈更生 / Chen Gengsheng

Pupils studying at night by candlelight at Lizhuang village, Yuanyang county of Central China's Henan province, on March 10, 1992.

1991年4月，安徽省六安市金寨县，照片的主人公苏明娟1983年出生在一个普通的农家，一家人过着辛劳拮据、朴素的生活，这张题为《我要上学》的照片发表后，被国内各大报纸争相转载并成为中国希望工程的宣传标志。

Hope in the eyes of Su Mingquan at Jinzhai county, East China's Anhui province in April 1991. This photo became a famous poster for Project Hope.

解海龙 / Xie Hailong

1984年，广东省深圳市，刚刚脱下军装的基建工程兵战士，在操场上进行军转工的技术晋级考试。

Service men from engineering corps of the People's Liberation Army take part in exams for new jobs immdiately after being demobilized in Shenzhen city, South China's Guangdong province, in 1984.

周顺斌 / Zhou Shunbin

1992年6月11日，云南省景洪县勐龙镇，按照傣家人的习俗，男孩到七八岁时都要出家受戒，在寺院里独立生活一段时间，几年后可以还俗。

冯 进 / Feng Jin

Trainee monks listen attentively during a lesson in Menglong town, Jinghong county of Southwest China's Yunnan province, on June 11, 1992. Boys of the Dai ethnic group aged 7 or 8 have to stay at a temple as monks before returning to secular life several years later.

2009年11月29日，山东省济南市天桥区，被人尊称为“流浪儿之父”的独身老人郑承镇与十个孩子的“全家福”。郑承镇收养的孩子中，有的读了大学上了警校，有的参军当兵。

吕廷川 / Lyu Tingchuan

Single old man Zheng Chengzhen has a photo taken with 10 orphans he has adopted on November 29, 2009. The 10 orphans have either entered university or joined army.

2002年6月9日，陕西省镇安县，该县遭遇了千年未遇的特大洪灾，县内多所小学受灾。为了不耽误孩子们的学习，镇安县黄家湾乡永红初小的刘洪兴老师，在废墟上给孩子们上课。

蔡 勇 / Cai Yong

A teacher giving a lesson in the open at Huangjiawan town, Zhen'an county of Northwest China's Shaanxi province on June 9, 2002 after a flood destroyed the primary school.

1991年10月，北京，少先队员们在治理凉水河的工地上参加义务劳动，孩子们的双手虽然稚嫩却干劲十足。

胡金喜 / Hu Jinxi

Pupils at work at the Liangshuihe River worksite in Beijing in October,1991.

1995年，内蒙古自治区东乌珠穆沁旗萨麦苏木，草原上，远处风吹草地见牛羊，近处孩子们笑脸盈盈。

车光照 / Che Guangzhao

Children in the Dong Ujimchin Banner, the Inner Monfgolia autonomous region, are all smiles for the camera, in 1995.

2007年7月2日，西藏自治区那曲市，双湖小学被资助的少年儿童，纯真的眼睛里闪烁着光芒。 丁 伟 / Ding Wei

Tibetan pupils are all smiles at Shuanghu Primary School, Nagchu city, the Tibet autonomous region, on July 2, 2007. The pupils had just received financial aid.

1998年，北京市东城区长巷胡同，两个小女孩在家门口吹长笛。

贾 勇 / Jia Yong

Girls play flutes in a lane in Beijing in 1998.

1995年12月6日，北京市海淀区，打工子弟学校的孩子们在好奇地看一台小相机。 刘新武 / Liu Xinwu

Pupils at a school for children of migrant workers in the suburbs of West Beijing in 1995.

2015年2月16日，四川省凉山彝族自治州，大凉山深处的美姑县，孩童们忘我地玩耍，这些孩子都将成为帮扶对象。

邱太建 / Qiu Taijian

Kids playing in Meigu county, Liangshan Yi autonomous prefecture of Southwest China's Sichuan province, on February 26, 2015.

2018年7月，广东省东莞市，参与美式橄榄球运动的青少年和他们的教练。

Chinese children playing Amercian football with their coach in Dongguan city, South China's Guandong province, in July, 2018.

何志高郎 / He Zhigaolang

2009年5月16日，澳门特别行政区，几名小学生攀爬倾斜的灯塔外立墙。

Kids climbing up a wall in Macao on May 16, 2009.

姜 建 / Jiang Jian

2016年1月，甘肃省临洮县，马家湾小学留守儿童王宝花把自己的心语写在黑板上，留守儿童问题一直备受社会各界关注。

任世琛 / Ren Shichen

A left-behind girl at Majiawan Primary School, Lintao county of West China's Gansu province, in January, 2016. Her parents have left her behind while they work in a city.

1995年7月8日，山东省济南市，一家人给刚满两周岁的四胞胎洗澡。

A family bathing two-year-old quadruplets in Ji'nan, East China's Shandong province, on July 8, 1995.

钱 捍 / Qian Han

1979年，孩子们游览北京故宫。

王文波 / Wang Wenbo

Tourists in the Forbidden City in Beijing in 1979.

2012年9月28日，陕西省咸阳市武功县，爷爷奶奶们每天准时在八一村村口，排队将孩子们送上幼儿园的校车，前往镇上读书学习。

Grandparents sending their grandchildren to school in Bayi village, Wugong county of Xianyang city in Northwest China's Shaanxi province, on September 28, 2012.

贾吉平 / Jia Jiping

2006年，陕西省西安市鼓楼，天文爱好者用天文望远镜观测天体。

惠怀杰 / Hui Huaijie

An astronomy lover looks into space through a telescope at the Drum Tower in downtown Xi'an, capital city of Northwest China's Shaanxi province, in 2006.

2014年7月11日，北京市永定门，教练带领学生们练习轮滑。　　刁立生 / Diao Lisheng

A coach teaching students rollerskating in front of Yongdingmen Tower Gate in Beijing on July 11, 2014.

2017年7月19日，海南省海口市，育婴员培训班教师通过实操课向学员讲解课程内容，吸引全省农民工、下岗职工、困难职工参加培训。

Free training on how to nurse new-born babies is provided at Haikou city, South China's Hainan province, on July 19, 2017.

袁　琛 / Yuan Chen

2018年7月7日，河北省张家口市张北县玉狗梁村，村民们在广场上练习瑜伽，此项运动给乡村增添了无限的活力，同时也改善了村民们的身体素质。

赵占南 / Zhao Zhannan

Villagers doing Yoga exercise at Yugouliang village, Zhangbei county of Zhangjiakou city in North China's Hebei province, on July 7, 2018.

1979年1月，北京市内燃机总厂，工人们在认真听技术讲座。

Workers listen attentatively during a lecture in a Beijing factory in January, 1979.

蒋 铎 / Jiang Duo

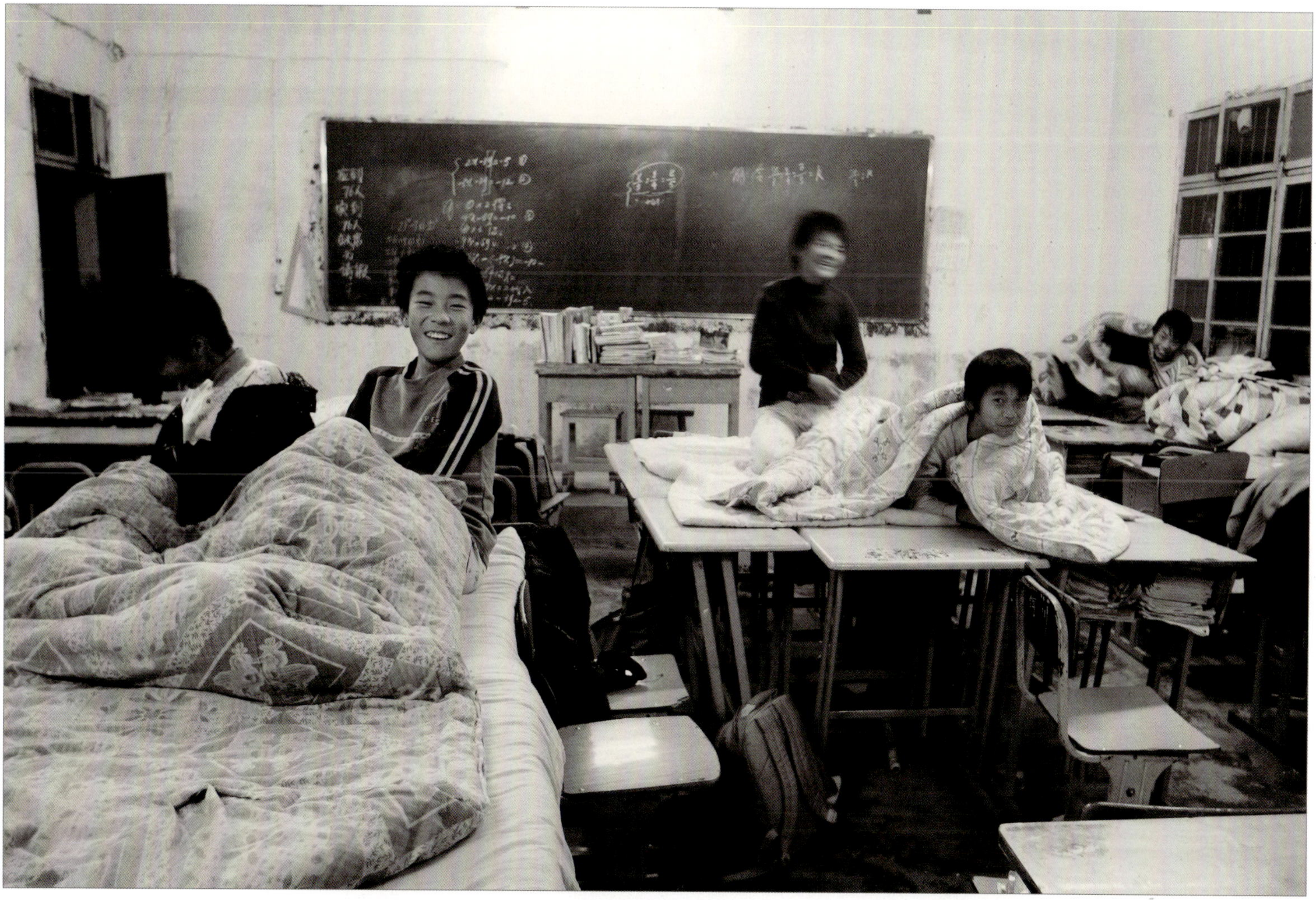

2010年12月5日，安徽省金寨县汤家汇中心学校的学生们，在宿舍楼翻修期间临时睡在教室里的书桌上。

陈 剑 / Chen Jian

Students prepare to sleep in a classroom at Tangjiahui Central Primary School at Jinzhai county, East China's Anhui province, on December 5, 2010. The old dormitory building was dilapidated and a new one was being constructed.

2017年12月30日，北京市王府井书店，小学生放学以后，沉浸在知识的海洋里。

Absorbed in books at Wangfujing Book Store on December 30, 2017.

刘建华 / Liu Jianhua

2015年11月21日，浙江省嘉兴市乌镇，木心美术馆。在这里，既有人沿袭传统纸质阅读方式，也有人喜好依靠手机互联网获取资讯。

耿菲菲 / Geng Feifei

Two visitors at Muxin Gallery in Wuzhen town, Jiaxing city of East China's Zhejiang province on November 21, 2015.

1995年7月9日，北京师范大学附属中学，高考第三天，众多家长在考场外翘首以待，迎接高考结束的孩子们。

卢北峰 / Lu Beifeng

Parents waiting outside the Experimental High School Attached to Beijing Normal University on July 9, 1997, the last day of the National College Entrance Examinations.

1984年10月，北京大学图书馆，坐满了认真学习的学生。

At the library of Peking University in October, 1984.

王文泉 / Wang Wenquan

1985年，北京市东城区汇文中学，物理老师余朝龙带领学生们上实践课。 崔新华 / Cui Xinhua

A teacher of physics with his students in Huiwen Middle School in Beijing in 1985.

1982年秋，山西省大同市左云县酸茨河乡，左云一中的苗补全出国留学，教室里挤满了前来交流的人们。

王　悦 / Wang Yue

In the autumn of 1982, Miao Buquan (in the middle) meets with his fellow villagers in Suancihe town, Zuoyun county of North China's Shanxi province, before going overseas to study. It was a big news in the town.

1987年5月28日，北京市海淀区，两弹一星功勋奖章获得者王淦昌院士，在北京科学会堂度过了80岁生日，他以科学报告的形式答谢对他的生日祝福。

Wang Ganchang, a scientist and academician of Chinese Academy of Sciences, on his 80-year-old birthday in Beijing on May 28, 1987.

罗更前 / Luo Gengqian

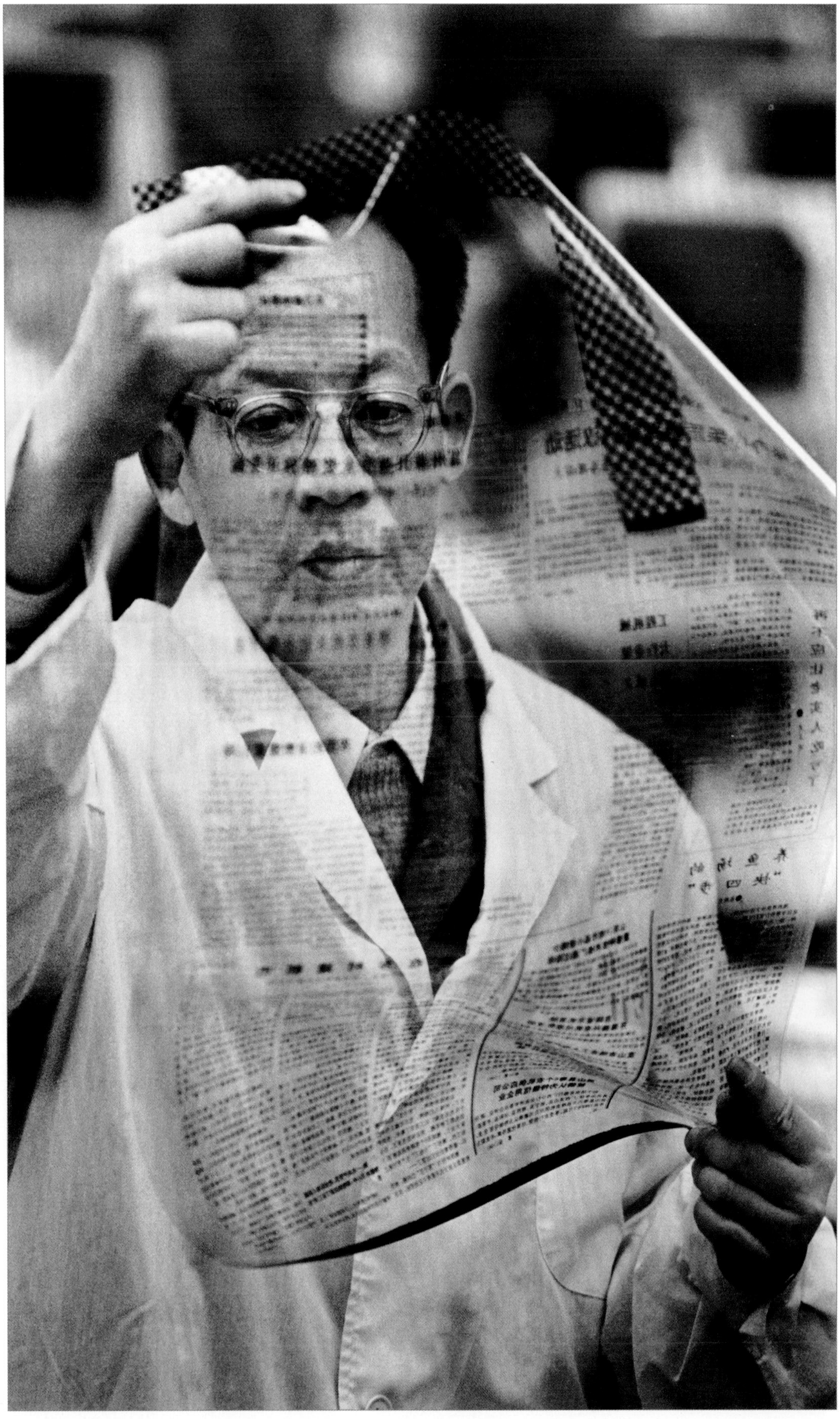

1990年3月，北京大学方正集团。王选是中国现代印刷革命奠基人，他所主持研制的汉字激光照排系统开创了汉字印刷的一个崭新时代。

Wang Xuan (1937-2006) looking at a photo film of a newspaper page in March, 1990. He was the father of Chinese character composition technology in China.

王文澜 / Wang Wenlan

2016年6月27日，四川省成都市，四川大学一位母亲带着孩子参加研究生毕业典礼。

陈元明 / Chen Yuanming

A boy looking at his mom during a postgraduate graduation ceremony at Sichuan University in Chengdu, Southwest China's Sichuan province, on June 27, 2016.

1984年初夏，广东省深圳市，在市总工会的职工夜校里，一位母亲带着儿子上夜大。

周顺斌 / Zhou Shunbin

A mother has her son with her while studing at a night school in Shenzhen city, South China's Guangdong province, in the early summer of 1984.

2016年6月，北京工业大学，电子信息工程学院211班的学子结束了四年本科教育，逸夫图书馆成为他们最留恋的校园一景。

张立杰 / Zhang Lijie

Graduates at the library in Beijing University of Technology before leaving the school in June, 2016.

2007年7月6日，北京大学，毕业典礼结束后，同学们来到校门口合影留念。

Having a photo taken at the gate of Peking University on July 6, 2007, after the graduation ceremony.

刘 慧 / Liu Hui

2018年6月26日，北京市海淀区，中国人民大学的毕业生在微信朋友圈特色主题的背景板后合影留念。

关 欣 / Guan Xin

A student at Renmin University of China in Beijing has her photo taken to celebrate her graduation on June 26, 2018.

2002年8月3日，北京人民大会堂，北京中加学校269名高中毕业生全部考取加拿大的高等院校。学生们出国留学前夕，学校举办了盛大欢快的毕业典礼。

Graduates from the Chinese-Canadian High School celebrate after their graduation ceremony in the Great Hall of the People on August 3, 2002. The students would study at Canadian universities.

张 风 / Zhang Feng

2015年11月，福建省龙海市，退休老人在公园里的台阶上阅读报纸。 徐 蕾 / Xu Lei

Elderly men read newspapers at a park in Longhai city, East China's Fujian province, in November, 2015.

1995年，北京市东城区，老年夜校吸引了许多前来求知的学员。 胡金喜 / Hu Jinxi

Elderly students in class at a night school for the elderly in Dongcheng District, Beijing, in 1995.

2012年9月3日，北京市朝阳区，望京体育广场，热爱唱歌的市民自发组成健康之声合唱团，丰富了退休老人们的业余生活。

何华藩 / He Huafan

A residents' choir singing at Wangjing Sport Square on September 3, 2012.

1980年12月6日，北京市，老战士、老干部和老知识分子在舞台上纵情歌唱。

贺延光 / He Yanguang

Veterns and intellectuals, many of whom had been politically persecuted during the "cultural revolution"(1966-76), singing their hearts out in Beijing on December 6, 1980.

1995年春节，上海市寅丰毛纺厂，在工友们的围观下，两个女孩跳起舞，增加节日气氛。

于文国 / Yu Wenguo

Workers enjoying dancing in a textile mill in Shanghai during Spring Festival in 1995.

1986年，北京市，披着军大衣的年轻人在街头跳舞。 郭建设 / Guo Jianshe

Young people dancing on the street in Beijing in 1986.

2016年8月15日，四川省康定市，甘孜监狱的服刑人员在操场上跳起了锅庄舞。 居 杨 / Ju Yang

Inmates dancing in the exercise yard of a prison in Kangding city, Southwest China's Sichuan province, on August 15, 2016.

1985年，四川省南充市，星期天在电影院旁学唱流行歌曲的人们。

杨　麾 / Yang Hui

People gather to sing popular songs on Sunday in Nanchong city, Southwest China's Sichuan province, in 1985.

2017年10月10日，陕西省西安市，古老的戏台上几位老人沉浸在华阴老腔的演出之中。

Elderly villagers absorbed in singing local Huayin Opera at an open stage in Xi'an, capital city of Northwest China's Shaanxi province, on October 10, 2017.

王宇澄 / Wang Yucheng

2018年4月27日，陕西省榆林市府谷县，当地剧团的演员们送戏下乡。

陆中秋 / Lu Zhongqiu

A local opera troupe on its way to a performance for rural villagers in Fugu county, Northwest China's Shaanxi province, on April 27, 2018.

1984年2月16日，陕西省西安市鄠邑区，深入农村的文艺工作者给农民送去文艺演出，休息期间，演员和当地群众拉家常。

An opera actor is chatting with a local villager during a break in Huyi district, Xi'an city, Northwest China's Shaanxi province on February 16,1984.

解海龙 / Xie Hailong

2015年3月，河北省定州市，百花梆子剧团下乡演出，演员们台下的闲暇趣味。 王东升 / Wang Dongsheng

Baihua Opera actors and actresses enjoying themselves after a performance in Dingzhou city, North China's Hebei province, in March, 2015.

2018年6月6日，北京市恭王府博物馆，“锦绣中华——中国非物质文化遗产服饰秀”系列活动在馆内开幕，秀场外，模特们谈笑风生，等候上场。

关 欣 / Guan Xin

Models wait their turn on the runway at a fashion show featuring intangible cultural heritage at the Palace of Prince Gong in Beijing on June 6, 2018.

2016年3月15日，北京地铁8号线，网络直播开始流行，主播在地铁车厢中做直播视频。

魏晓昊/ Wei Xiaohao

An internet program anchor person doing live streaming on subway Line 8 on March 15, 2016, in Beijing.

2018年4月14日，北京市，小丑艺人李克文在出租屋里通过网络直播表演杂耍、魔术。随着互联网的飞速发展，越来越多的人选择加入主播大军，开启直播生涯。

邹 红 / Zou Hong

Forty-six-year-old clown Li Kewen livestreaming his performance from a room he rented in Beijing on April 14, 2018.

惠怀杰 / Hui Huaijie

2009年，陕西省延安市安塞区，安塞腰鼓秧歌队的成员们集体合影。
安塞腰鼓的磅礴气势和出众的表现力令人陶醉，堪称“天下第一鼓”。

Waist drum dancers have a photo taken in Ansai district, Yan'an city, Northwest China's Shaanxi province, in 2009.

2012年，江苏省无锡市，老年合唱队在锡惠公园里吹拉弹唱，不亦乐乎。 席建南 / Xi Jiannan

A choir of elderly residents enjoy themselves at Xihui Park in Wuxi city, East China's Jiangsu province in 2012.

2018年6月，北京市密云区古北水镇，女性身穿旗袍亮相。 何志高郎 / He Zhigaolang

A *qipao* show at Gubei Water Town, Miyun district, Beijing, in June, 2018.

2010年，陕西省西安市鄠邑区，两代女性并肩而行。

胡武功 / Hu Wugong

In these elderly women's eyes, how fashionable these young women look in Huyi district, Xi'an, capital of Northwest China's Shaanxi province in 2010.

2016年，北京市东城区天坛公园，舞蹈爱好者跳水兵舞。

李云鸿 / Li Yunhong

Women line dancing at the Temple of Heaven in Beijing in 2016.

1989年，北京市东城区，地坛公园里跳迪斯科的老年人。

张兆增 / Zhang Zhaozeng

Elderly people dancing in Ditan Park, Beijing, in 1989.

2014年10月17日，北京市天坛公园，双胞胎姊妹现代舞演员，身着一黑一白，即兴表演双人舞。

郭延民 / Guo Yanmin

Two ballerinas at the Temple of Heaven in Beijing on October 17, 2014.

1995年，北京市，15岁的杨春红和13岁的赵娜在练习高车踢碗，她们苦练3年，凭借精湛的技艺，在国内外登台献艺。

李 楠 / Li Nan

Two are practicing acrobatic stunts in Beijing in 1995. They both later performed in the Great Hall of the People and even overseas.

2014年4月2日，北京市，中央芭蕾舞团在天桥剧场演出芭蕾舞剧《仙女》，身形婀娜的舞蹈演员们即将上场演出。

Ballerinas prepare to go on stage at Tianqiao Theater in Beijing on April 2, 2014.

刘 阳 / Liu Yang

2007年12月1日，海南省三亚市，第57届世界小姐大赛全球总决赛，中国的职业模特张梓琳从全世界一百多名参赛选手中脱颖而出，获得冠军。

Miss World Zhang Zilin in Sanya, South China's Hainan province, on December 1, 2007. She was the first Chinese to win the Miss World title.

刘占坤 / Liu Zhankun

2009年11月14日，第49届国际小姐大会总决赛的70多名“美丽使者”访问北京加拿大国际学校。她们挥动毛笔，书写和平、友爱的美好愿望。

陆中秋 / Lu Zhongqiu

Participants in the 49th Miss International Competition write Chinese calligraphy at Canadian International School of Beijing on November 14, 2009.

2016年4月16日，北京国际时装周，中国小伙扶起跌倒的模特。

常 江 / Chang Jiang

A Chinese youth extending a helping hand to a model after she falls at a fashion show in Beijing on April 16, 2016.

2006年4月1日，北京市东城区，中国第一商业街王府井，模特亮相中国首场内衣艺术视觉展“梦幻伊甸”。 毛建军 / Mao Jianjun

Modeling underwear at a fashion show in Beijing on April 1, 2006.

2005年7月28日，北京市东城区，“仲夏法兰西——北京”在中国美术馆布展，工作人员在悬挂重400斤、价值高达75亿元的《跨越阿尔卑斯山圣伯纳隘道的拿破仑》巨幅油画。

邹 红 / Zou Hong

A painting of Napoleon I being hung for an exhibition at National Art Museum of China in Beijing on July 28, 2005.

2018年7月，山东省青岛市，一位身穿蓝色裙子的女孩正在充满艺术感的楼梯上拍摄时尚照片。

A woman has a photo taken with a dramatic staircase as the backdrop in Qingdao city, East China's Shandong province, in July, 2018.

张桐胜 / Zhang Tongsheng

2007年，香港特别行政区，三个时尚女青年用一张人脸图片拍摄趣味合影。

王　苗 / Wang Miao

A photo taken for three girls in Hong Kong in 2007.

2010年5月4日，上海市，世博园内来自不同国家的100多名志愿者共同完成了名为“敞开您的微笑”的作品。

黑　克 / Hei Ke

Volunteers from different countries at the Shanghai World Expo on May 4, 2010.

2015年9月25日，河南省郑州市上街区，随着中国航空事业的发展，各地开展起规模盛大的航展活动。孩子们在郑州航展上展示他们的“特技飞行”。

牟健为 / Mou Jianwei

Children frolic at a air show in Zhengzhou, capital city of Central China's Henan province, on September 25, 2015.

1991年11月，北京前门，胡同里的一个女孩在玩呼啦圈。

A girl plays with a hola hoop in Beijing in November, 1991.

黄小兵 / Huang Xiaobing

2017年4月21日，北京市丰台区，意馨艺术幼儿园三路居分园开展家长半日观摩活动，一位父亲与孩子共同参与趣味体育游戏，活动现场其乐融融。

新吉乐夫 / Xinjilefu

A father and son participate in a sports program at a kindergarten in Beijing on April 21, 2017.

2013年9月20日，北京市赵府街，玩“推车游戏”的孩子们。

张 洁 / Zhang Jie

Boys playing a game in Zhaofujie Lane, Beijing, on September 20, 2013.

2018年4月，四川省凉山彝族自治州，一群在篮球场上奋力投篮的少年。

李铁强 / Li Tieqiang

A basketball game in Liangshan Yi autonomous prefecture, Southwest China's Sichuan province, in April, 2018.

2004年10月4日，北京市宣武区，胡同里的孩子们在简易篮筐下投篮。

Pupils play basketball in a lane in Beijing on October 4, 2004.

刁立生 / Diao Lisheng

2015年5月16日，江苏省连云港市，孩子们练习花式足球。

谷 晶 / Gu Jing

Students at a football training class in Lianyungang city, East China's Jiangsu province, on May 16, 2015.

2018年3月20日，吉林省白山市浑江区八一希望学校，体育教师赵政军带领幼儿园的孩子们上足球课。

王丽莺 / Wang Liying

Kids from a kindergarten are having a football class on a local campus in Hunjiang district, Baishan city of Northeast China's Jilin province, on March 20, 2018.

2009年4月12日，西藏自治区那曲市双湖县多玛乡，藏族小学生在踢足球，稚嫩的脸上难掩喜悦与兴奋。

车刚 / Che Gang

Students having fun with a football at Duoma town, Shuanghu county of Nagchu city in the Tibet autonomous region, on April 12, 2009.

2008年，云南省西双版纳傣族自治州勐海县，课余时间，身穿袈裟的小和尚们踢足球。

孙大虹 / Sun Dahong

Little monks are playing football after school in Menghai county, Xishuangbanna Dai autonomous prefecture, Yunnan province, in 2018,.

2017年6月，河南省嵩山少林寺，几位认真学习中国功夫的“洋弟子”。

Foreign children practising martial arts at Shaolin Temple in Central China's Henan province in June, 2017.

李铁强 / Li Tieqiang

少

1986年，浙江省淳安县，农民们下工后打台球，随着改革开放，农民的休闲娱乐生活变得多姿多彩。

吴宗其 / Wu Zongqi

Billiards is a popular pastime for local rural villagers in Chun'an county, East China's Zhejiang province, in 1986.

1992年10月，陕西省延安市，一个外国女孩在人们的围观下打台球。 王文扬 / Wang Wenyang

A shot on a street in Yan'an city, Northwest China's Shaanxi province in October, 1992.

1989年4月，北京市东单公园，人们练习踢花毽。

康泰森 / Kang Taisen

A shuttlecock game in Dongdan Park in Beijing in April, 1989.

2017年10月5日，陕西省西安市，太极拳团队深入秦岭山中，体验人与大自然的浑然一体。

赵利军 / Zhao Lijun

A shadow boxing team from Chang'an district, Northwest China's Shaanxi province, are exercising deep in Qinling Mountain on October 5, 2017.

2010年，吉林省大安市嫩江湾，活跃着一支40多人组成的业余冬泳队，年龄最大的队员有68岁，他们每次下水前都要在自制的器械上热身。

王野村 / Wang Yecun

Warming up before jumping into freezing water for winter swimming at Nenjiang River in Da'an city, Northeast China's Jilin province in 2010.

2015年4月26日，北京市朝阳区九龙山路街心花园，钢管舞培训中心的学员们正在训练表演，钢管舞已经成为年轻人喜闻乐见的健身时尚运动。

孙正懿 / Sun Zhengyi

At a pole dance training class in a park at Shuangjing subdistrict, Chaoyang district in Beijing, on April 26, 2015.

1990年，北京市海淀区，假日里，人们来到玉渊潭公园，在“八一湖”边消暑纳凉，准备下水游泳。

In the scorching summer of 1990, people swarm to the lake in Yuyuantan Park in Beijing to cool themselves.

刘 宇 / Liu Yu

2014年5月17日，福建省南平市，江滨公园一群爱好象棋的人们围绕在一棵大树下观棋，市民们称之为“娱乐圈”。

范崇智 / Fan Chongzhi

Playing chess in Jiangbin Park in Nanping city, East China's Fujian province, on May 17, 2014.

2017年5月10日，四川省江油市青莲镇大宝村，田园风光，绿意盎然，人们在花海中骑行。 刘丽华 / Liu Lihua

A ride among flowers at Dabao village, Qinglian town, Jiangyou city in Southwest China's Sichuan province, on May 10, 2017.

2015年3月8日，广东省深圳市，中国首届女子马拉松赛开跑，赛事分为：“全程组”42.195公里，“半程组”21公里，“体验组”5.5公里，来自国内外的3000余名女性跑者掀起了美丽的运动旋风。

吴 峻 / Wu Jun

China's first marathon for women in Shenzhen, South China's Guangdong province, on March 8, 2015.

2008年9月17日，北京市朝阳区，残奥会闭幕后，并肩作战了一个多月的志愿者们，在“鸟巢”体育场里欢呼雀跃，合影留念。

牛宏超 / Niu Hongchao

Volunteers for Beijing Paralympics celebrate the end of the games in Beiing on September 17, 2008.

2014年9月27日，上海市浦东新区，在东方体育中心参加彩色健康跑的运动员从起点出发。

Runners start a race from the Oriental Sports Center in Shanghai on September 27, 2014.

范筱明 / Fan Xiaoming

THE COLOR RUN.
296
2720

非常荣幸能够再次参与由中国日报社发起的“百名摄影师聚焦”项目。这是特想集团与中国日报社的第八次合作。“百名摄影师聚焦项目”作为中国摄影界知名品牌，从2003年至今，已出版16本画册，成为一个向世界真实、立体展示中国的窗口，享誉海内外。

我是上个世纪五十年代出生的人，亲身经历了中国改革开放四十年的整个过程。过去的四十年，是不断深化改革的四十年，是不断深化开放的四十年，也是全国共同奋进的四十年，而且是全球性的奋进。

在这四十年中，香港和澳门深受改革开放的影响：国内超十亿人口的市场打开，尤其是南方地区的制造业，如雨后春笋般涌现，“中国制造”的价廉物美的商品，迅速占领欧美百货、零售店，刺激了国内进出口业的发展，世界各大知名品牌纷纷以北京、上海、深圳等一线城市为根据地百花齐放，发展迅猛。

我常常在全球各地出差，四十年来的改革开放带来的国际影响更是明显。从2000年开始，中国游客海外旅行日益便利，无论是机场、街道、大小食肆，还是酒店、商店，都有中文标识，大街小巷，红绿灯旁，普通话处处可闻。同时，我在国内也常见外国朋友积极学习中国文化，其普通话之流利、发音之准确甚至让大部分南方人感到汗颜。

一切都在短短的四十年内发生。成长、改变，再成长、再改变，大时代背景下科技飞速发展，拉动整个改革开放取得辉煌成果，从绿铁皮火车到今天的“复兴号”高铁，从桌上的有线电话到掌中的智能手机等等，都展示了改革开放的巨大成就。

中国现在已是大国、强国，我学养不深，不敢随意置评，但对上世纪五十年代出生、经历过整个四十年改革开放过程并有海内外亲身经验的我来说，我真心赞叹改革开放的巨大力量，它改变了很多人的生活，改变了很多人的人生。

让我们一起祝福中国的将来永远美好，愿改革开放取得更大的发展成果！

刘绚强
永洪集团、特想集团
董事长

劉绚强

It is a great honor for me to be able to participate in the "100 photographers focus" program initiated by China Daily. It is the eighth time for the Wink Impression Co Ltd to cooperate with China Daily. As a well-known photography collection brand in the industry, 16 "focus" albums have been published since 2003, and they have become a window showcasing China in a multi-dimensional manner.

Born in the 1950s, I have witnessed the implementation of reform and opening-up over the past four decades, during which reform has been constantly deepened, opening up constantly furthered and the Chinese people have constantly made endeavors in all fields, endeavors that have remained globally oriented.

Over the past four decades, Hong Kong and Macao have been greatly impacted by mainland's reform and opening-up. A huge market involving a population of more than 1 billion was opened up. The manufacturing industry in South China boomed rapidly and "made-in-China" entered shopping malls and retail outlets around the world, which has stimulated the import and export industries in China. At the same time, world brands have made their way into China's big cities such as Beijing, Shanghai and Shenzhen.

I've traveled all over the world, and seen how China's reform and opening-up have had an impact on the world. Starting from 2000, it has become increasingly convenient for Chinese tourists to travel globally, signboards in Chinese are everywhere in airports, streets, restaurants, hotels and shopping malls. Putonghua can be heard everywhere. I have met a lot of foreigners who can speak fluent Chinese and many more who were enthusiastically learning Chinese.

Many changes have taken place over the past 40 years. The rapid development of science and technology has added to what the reform and opening-up have achieved. High-speed railways and smartphones epitomize the great achievements made by reform and opening-up, not least in the way they have transformed people's lives.

China is a large and strong power. I am not in the position to comment. However, as a man who was born in the 1950s and who has witnessed four decades of reform and opening-up with domestic and overseas experience, I sincerely hail what reform and opening-up have achieved, which has changed the lives of many.

Let's wish China an even more beautiful future and reform and opening-up even greater achievements!

Liu Xuanqiang

Chairman of Wing Hung Group
Chairman of Wink Group

1978年，中国迎来了改革开放的历史时刻。中国人民自强不息，情怀激荡，无数奋斗故事感动着我们。今年是改革开放四十周年，一个欣欣向荣的新时代的中国，正在实现中华民族伟大复兴的道路上阔步前进。

中国日报社发起的“百名摄影师聚焦中国改革开放四十年”活动，回顾过去，放眼未来，全方位讲述中国故事，展现了改革开放四十年来中国人民取得的伟大成就。北京中加学校（及十六所各地中加学校），北京加拿大国际学校（及四所各地国际学校）非常荣幸能够再次参与“百名摄影师聚焦”项目，与中国日报社共同打造这本画册，希望画册可以让大家看到时间通过摄影作品所体现的力量，并充分了解中国改革开放的生动故事。

北京中加学校成立二十余年以及北京加拿大国际学校成立十二年来，始终坚持“国际化、专业化、个性化”的内涵式发展思路，在“教育面向现代化、面向世界、面向未来”的征程中，走出了一条“放眼全球、融合中外，文化融合、贯通古今，课程互建，资源共享，促进学生健康成长，生动活泼主动学习，不拘一格育人才”的办学之路。和“百名摄影师聚焦”项目已走过的十五年历程一样，我们都在改革开放中上下求索，以砥砺奋进的姿态，参与、见证中华民族的复兴。

最后，我谨代表北京中加学校与所有国内师生，北京加拿大国际学校所有外教及在华外籍人员子女，向《百名摄影师聚焦中国改革开放四十年》画册顺利出版表示衷心祝贺，向摄影师和画册编辑团队表示敬意！

祝福中国！感谢新时代！

彭建华
加拿大加皇国际教育集团
董事长

Many stories have had a strong appeal to our sentiment since the reform and opening-up was initiated in 1978. A prosperous China is well on the way to its great rejuvenation as it celebrates the 40th anniversary of its reform and opening-up.

The China Daily photo album *100 Photographers Focus on Forty Years of Reform and Opening-Up* traced the country's changes over the past 40 years and looks toward the future. The stories these photos tell are representative of what China has achieved in the past four decades. It is an honor for Beijing Concord College of Sino-Canada (including all its branches in China) and Canadian International School of Beijing (including four such schools in the rest of China) to participate in this program. We hope that readers will appreciate more the profound impact China's reform and opening-up have had on the country and on people's lives by looking through this album.

Beijing Concord College of Sino-Canada has maintained the orientation of internationalization, professionalization and its own characteristics in the past more than two decades since its founding and so has Canadian International School of Beijing in the past 12 years since its launch in China. In their endeavors to provide modernized, globalized and future-oriented education, both schools have blazed a trail of their own, one characterized by a global vision, integration of both Chinese and foreign culture, the combining of both ancient and contemporary knowledge and the sharing of all resources. In so doing, both schools try to make it possible for students to develop in a healthy manner. In the 15 years we have cooperated with this album program, we have all participated in and witnessed the process of this country's rejuvenation.

On behalf of both schools in China and their faculty, as well as the students, we sincerely congratulate the publication of this album and give our best wishes to all photographers and editors.

Best wishes for China and for this new era.

Francis Pang

Chairman of AKD International Inc

Dr. Francis Pang

图书在版编目（CIP）数据

百名摄影师聚焦中国改革开放四十年 / 王浩主编. --北京:中国文联出版社, 2018.10

ISBN 978-7-5190-3948-6

Ⅰ.①百… Ⅱ.①王… Ⅲ.①改革开放－成就－中国－摄影集

Ⅳ. ①D619-64

中国版本图书馆 CIP 数据核字(2018)第 233480 号

百名摄影师聚焦中国改革开放四十年

作　　者：王　浩

出 版 人：朱　庆

终 审 人：奚耀华　　复 审 人：王柏松

责任编辑：王东升　王素珍　　责任校对：邢　宇

封面设计：新吉乐夫　　责任印制：陈　晨

出版发行：中国文联出版社

地　　址：北京市朝阳区农展馆南里 10 号，100125

电　　话：010-85923016（咨询）85923000（编务）85923020（邮购）

传　　真：010-85923000（总编室），010-85923020（发行部）

网　　址：http://www.clapnet.cn　　http://www.claplus.cn

E - mail：clap@clapnet.cn　　wangds@clapnet.cn

印　　刷：深圳市德信美印刷有限公司

装　　订：深圳市德信美印刷有限公司

法律顾问：北京市德鸿律师事务所王振勇律师

本书如有破损、缺页、装订错误，请与本社联系调换

开　　本：787×1092　　1/12

字　　数：42千字　　印 张：32.5

版　　次：2018 年 10 月第 1 版　　印 次：2018 年 10 月第 1 次印刷

书　　号：ISBN 978-7-5190-3948-6

定　　价：298.00 元